Trap Making
Step by Step

Detailed plans for professionals gamekeepers and smallholders

By
John Bryan

This book is dedicated to my Mum and Dad.

My thanks also go to all those helped in the creation of this book;
through proof reading, discussion, design testing
and good old fashioned encouragement.

Measure twice, cut once and don't cut the 'leaving on piece' off.

ISBN: 978-0-9558535-0-0

Chapter 1 - Introduction

The traps in this book are traditional ones and have been used for many years in one form or another. They are often featured in books as pictures or diagrams but rarely with all of the practical details necessary to build them.

This book is written for those people who want to build their own traps and will provide readers with a springboard for their own ideas. Specific plans for several traps are provided and these can be followed step by step by anyone using basic woodwork tools. Options and alternatives are included so that even these designs can be adapted and developed by readers. By the end of the book the plans are more flexible and allow the reader to finalise the details themselves using techniques learned earlier in the book.

It is always worth reading each chapter through to the end before you start any preparation. Many of the options and variations require building in from an early stage and it can be frustrating to discover this after you've cut the wood.

Trap Types

Box Traps are all structurally similar being based on a long box; sometimes 'blind', (meaning blocked at one end) and other times 'tunnels' open all the way through. However the many variations on doors, locks and triggers add to the flexibility and interest of these traps which are commonly used to capture small mammals. Box traps are usually baited, but not always, and where bait is used it serves partly to attract quarry but often as a means of triggering the trap as well.

You can also make box traps from heavy gauge weld mesh and many of the ideas around doors and triggers are transferable with the wooden ones. In comparison though the 'All Mesh' traps have the advantages of being light weight, rot proof and provide full visibility inside. Being bright and open, mesh traps of the right design are also suitable for birds, which would be reluctant to enter a dark tunnel. Ironically it is this tunnel effect which is so attractive to mammals and so mesh traps for these must generally be disguised with vegetation or natural debris.

Frame and Mesh traps are generally medium to very large, multi-catch traps made from a wooden or metal frame covered in chicken wire or similar wire mesh. They are light, airy, open structures designed to attract and capture birds. The best designs are made up from separate panels that can be assembled on site but dismantled for transport or repair. These traps have minimal moving parts and capture by means of restricted access allowing birds to drop or walk in but not fly out. The Larsen Trap is the exception that proves the rule - it is a frame and mesh structure but smaller and has two sprung trap doors.

If you are unfamiliar with any particular trap I strongly advise you to read through the whole chapter before you make a start. Have a look at the website (www.fourteenacre.co.uk) listed in the 'Further Resources' chapter. This site includes multiple photographs which will help you to visualise what you're making.

Legal and Moral Responsibilities

Anyone considering making and using any traps from this book must be aware of the law in their geography and be prepared to deal with any successful catches. Traps must be inspected regularly and at least daily, I recommend twice a day. Any catches should be either released or humanely killed and disposed of appropriately. It is unacceptable to prolong the suffering of any animal regardless of how much it may be regarded as a 'pest'. A cheap air rifle or an air pistol is an excellent tool for close range dispatch of captured target animals.

Magpies and pigeons can be effectively and humanely killed by a sharp blow to the back of the head with a short, heavy stick known as a 'priest'. You should be holding the bird with one hand so that the blow is accurate and instant – it is not good enough to just swing at the birds and hope to hit them correctly.

As a basic safety precaution gloves should be worn as rats, in particular, can carry potentially fatal disease. Wherever possible you should avoid handling most animals altogether.

Trappers must be familiar with the animals being targeted and be able to distinguish them from any which may be caught accidentally. By default UK law protects all birds and animals and only allowing specific exceptions. For example there are currently few restrictions on catching rats, mice, grey squirrels or rabbits. However Grey squirrel are a non-native species and if caught must be humanely killed as it is an offence to release them back into the wild. Conversely Red Squirrels are protected; they must be released unharmed if caught and if accidentally caught regularly trapping should be stopped in that area.

The control of magpies, crows and woodpigeons is restricted by law and is only permitted under specific general licences published annually by Natural England (http://www.naturalengland.org.uk/conservation) and The Scottish Executive for Scotland (www.scottishexecutive.gov.uk). These licences are automatically available to everyone - there is no need to apply for them. However they relate to specific reasons and circumstances so you must understand them, comply with them and keep up to date with changes.

The most commonly used licences are:

Licence to kill or take certain birds to conserve wild birds.
Licence to kill or take certain birds to preserve public health or public safety
Licence to kill or take certain birds to prevent serious damage or disease (damage to livestock, foodstuffs for livestock, crops, vegetables, fruit, growing timber, fisheries or inland waters)

Take the time to find out the law for where you live.

General Terms, Materials and Techniques

Materials

The traps in this book are made using three main materials; plywood, roofing lath and wire mesh.

- Roofing Lath is the long timber strips used across roof beams to support the tiles. Typically 35mm wide by 18mm thick, this tanalsed pine is sold in lengths of 2.4m or 4.8m from any timber yard or builders merchant. Being pressure treated it is already weather resistant and ideal for outdoor use.
- Where plywood is used it must be external grade, or even better marine grade. Although manufactured for outdoor use, plywood is a composite material and so has lots of gaps where moisture can get in and start to damage it. Plywood will always benefit from a couple of coats of preservative such as Cuprinol. Avoid strong smelling creosote at all costs as this will keep animals away for months.
- Wire mesh should be galvanised and about 19g unless otherwise stated. For some applications plastic coated wire would also be suitable although plain plastic garden netting is not. Care should also be taken to select the correct mesh size and if in any doubt go smaller rather than larger. Rats and squirrels can comfortably fit though a 2 inch hole and will often pass through smaller ones. Mesh of the wrong size can also increase the chances of trapped animals injuring themselves.

Terms & Techniques

'Starting off' nails	This means hammering a nail part way through a piece of wood to get it 'started off' before getting all the pieces lined up. The advantage is that this gets the nails firmly in position so it's easier when you come to the final assembly.
Starter holes	Starter holes are a shallow holes made with a bradawl or similar that make it easier to start screws or screw fittings like screw eyes.
Pilot holes & Counter Sinks Counter Sink · Pilot Hole	Pilot holes are narrow diameter holes drilled in preparation for screws or nails to avoid splitting the wood. A counter sink is a small conical hole to allow the head of a screw or bolt to become level with the wood surface.

Tools

There are some basic tools which you really can't do without for these projects. Nothing too expensive and you probably have most of them at home already.

- **Workbench.**
  Most important of all is somewhere to work. It doesn't have to be anything special and one of those fold-away workbenches available in DIY shops is ideal to start with. Any table or bench will do as long as it is level, stable and a comfortable working height.
- **Hammer.**
  Preferably a 'claw' hammer – the type with the two prongs on the back for removing nails.
- **Saw.**
  A good quality cross-cut wood saw - there's nothing worse for trying to cut neat, straight lines than a cheap, blunt saw.
- **Screwdriver.**
  Make sure that it's suitable for the screws you are going to use (i.e. slot or cross head).
- **Carpenters Square.**
  This is something you might not have but well worth getting. It's a standard carpenter's tool used for marking lines at right angles to the edges of wood.
- **Marking Gauge**
  Another carpenter's tool, this device is for marking lines parallel to the edge of a piece of wood. Again something you may not have but inexpensive and you'll wonder how you ever managed without one.
- **Coping Saw.**
  A saw with a thin blade held in between the arms of a 'U' shaped frame. This type of saw is used for cutting out shapes in solid pieces of wood. If you already have a jigsaw then that already does the job.
- **Wire Cutters.**
  Nothing too heavy-duty just suitable for cutting the wire mesh.
- **Drill.**
  A hand or electric drill with a range of drill bits.
- **Bradawl.**
  A short pointed spike mounted in a handle – used to make starter holes for screws.
- **Staple Gun.**
  Not strictly essential but you'll find it much easier with one. A handheld staple gun will allow you to fix mesh quickly and neatly with one hand while positioning the mesh with the other.

There are also a few other project specific tools given at the start of some chapters.

Chapter 2 – The Drop Top box trap

I first saw this trap in the book 'Camp Life in the Woods and the Tricks of Trapping and Trap Making' by William Hamilton Gibson published in 1870 (see Further Resources). It makes an excellent first project.

The basic principle is that the lid and front of the trap are pivoted and suspended above the trapping chamber. A length of cord holds them up, runs over the raised back of the trap and is tied to a short spindle. The weight of the lid creates tension on the cord, which in turn holds the spindle against a pair of pegs. One of these pegs is fixed, the other is a long rod which passes through a loose hole into the body of the trap and has bait attached.

To an animal this trap looks airy, open and relatively safe. Any attempt to remove the bait will dislodge the baited peg. This will release the spindle, free the cord and drop the trap lid closed.

The original design presents the trapper with a closed box with no way to determine what is caught. The modified design on the following pages includes a mesh inspection panel.

This trap is suitable for many small mammals and can be made in various sizes as described in the table on the next page. Conceivably it could even be used to catch foxes although I have never tried it for anything as large as that.

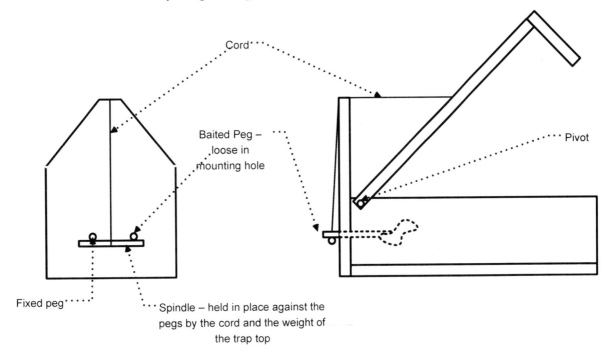

Cord

Baited Peg – loose in mounting hole

Pivot

Fixed peg

Spindle – held in place against the pegs by the cord and the weight of the trap top

Cutting List & Materials

- 12mm exterior grade plywood sizes as shown
- 4mm steel rod axle—length 'C'
- 3 x screw eyes (17mm long, 5mm hole diameter)
- Strong, light, rot proof cord of length 'C' + 'E'. Preferable not brightly coloured
- 8mm dowel of length C
- Section of wire mesh 'D' by 'C'.
- 30mm wire nails

Tools

- Saw
- Hammer
- Drill with 3.5 mm & 4mm bit
- Screwdriver
- Bradawl
- Jigsaw or coping saw
- Wood plane or sandpaper

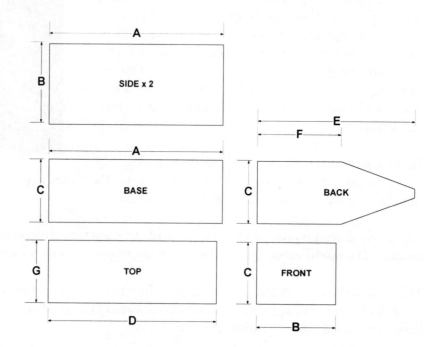

Timber sizes in mm (in)	A	B	C	D	E	F	G
Squirrel / Rat	460mm (18 in)	130mm (5 in)	150mm (6 in)	448mm (17 ½in)	280mm (11 in)	142mm (5 ½ in)	121mm (4 ¾ in)
Rabbit	510mm (20 in)	230mm (9 in)	180mm (7 in)	498mm (19 ½in)	400mm (16 in)	242mm (9 ½ in)	150 mm (5 ¾ in)
Mouse	155mm (6 in)	100mm (4 in)	100mm (4 in)	143mm (5 ½in)	170mm (6 ¾ in)	112mm (4 ½ in)	71mm (2 ¾ in)

Assembly instructions

Making the Top

1 Take the 'top' piece and mark two large circles, roughly in the centre of each 'half'. They don't have to be circles – any shape will do but don't go closer than 25mm (1 in) to any edge and don't make the shapes too complicated.

2 Using a jigsaw or coping saw carefully cut out these shapes. If you have a 'core drill' then you can just use that to cut holes straight away as we don't need the removed piece.

3 Mark two points 13mm (½ in) in from one end and 25mm (1in) in from either side. Use a bradawl or large nail to start holes at these points and then fit the screw eyes. Finish with them inline as a pair across the width to form part of the axle.

4 Lay mesh over the openings and secure with staples.

5 Turn the top over

6 Fit one screw eye in the centre of the top, between the meshed holes.

Mesh attached on underside

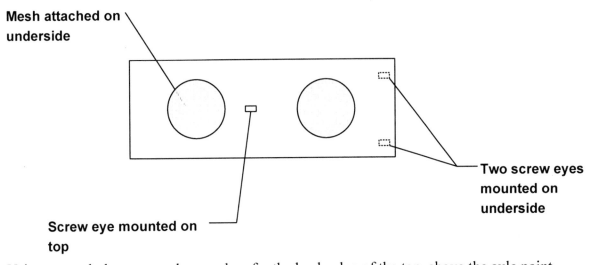

Two screw eyes mounted on underside

Screw eye mounted on top

7 Using a wood plane or sandpaper chamfer the back edge of the top, above the axle point. This will reduce the chances of the top catching on the back of the trap when opening or closing.

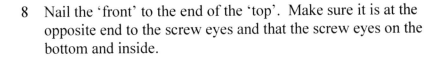

8 Nail the 'front' to the end of the 'top'. Make sure it is at the opposite end to the screw eyes and that the screw eyes on the bottom and inside.

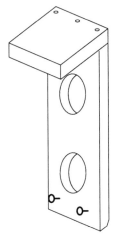

Making the Box

9 Take one side and mark a point in one corner, 18mm (¾ in) in from each edge. Drill a 4mm hole right through.

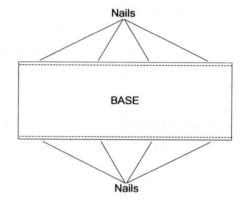

10 Put the two side pieces together and ensure that they are lined up exactly on all edges. Ideally clamp them together in a vice to prevent any movement, then using the first hole as a guide drill through the second piece.

11 Next take the base board and mark a line about 6mm (³/₁₆ in) in from each of the long edges. Take 6 to 8 nails, (half along each side), and at roughly equal intervals start the nails off along the marked lines.

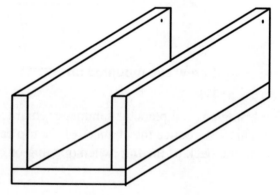

12 Stand the two sides edge down on the bench and about the right distance apart. Check that the two holes you drilled are opposite each other and near the downward edge. Place the base board on top, nails up. Carefully line up one side with the base and hammer in the nails for that side. Then repeat for the other side. Turn over and you will have the basic box shape

13 **Take the Rear Section**

Lay the rear section on the bench and mark two points – 60mm (2 ¼ in) up from the base and 50mm (2 in) in from each side.

14 Drill two holes; one diameter 7.5 mm to tightly hold the fixed peg and the second diameter 8.5 mm to take the bait peg. Cut a 25mm (1 in) length of dowel and gently knock this into the fixed peg hole. It should not stick out the other side and there should be about 12mm (½ in) remaining.

15 Insert a screw eye in the centre of the short, flat top.

16 Start nails along the bottom and up the straight sides.

17 Stand the main box on its front (that is with the axle holes upwards). Position the rear section and nail it on.

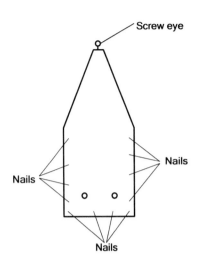

Fitting the Trap Top

18 Stand the box up on the rear section. Put the top roughly into position and hold it open so that you can see inside.

19 Push the steel bar through the hole in one side of the box, pass it through the screw eyes under the top and out though the hole on the other side of the box.

20 Check that the top opens and closes freely. If it doesn't then remove the bar and the top chamfer a bit more off the back edge if that's where it's catching.

Fitting the Trigger

21 Take the remaining length of dowel and cut it into two pieces; a 90mm (3 ½ in) spindle and a 180mm (7") trigger. Lift the lid with one hand; take the trigger in the other and from inside the trap push it through the remaining hole in the back board.

22 Tie one end of the cord securely to the screw eye in the trap top. Pass the cord through the screw eye in the top edge of the rear section and allow it to hang down between the two pegs.

23 Prop the top of the trap open at an angle about 60 degrees and gently pull the cord tight. Mark the cord at the length where it is level with the pegs and tie on the spindle. Put the spindle under the pegs and gently release the trap top. Adjust as necessary and then trim off any excess cord

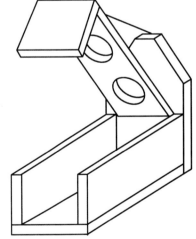

Options and variations

Alternative Triggers

Variation on this basic trigger mechanism, and many other triggers types can be found by following the 'further resources' list included at the end of this book.

Weights and Springs

These traps would have originally been made from 25mm (1 in) thick planks of seasoned hardwood and the weight of the lid alone would have been enough. By comparison, modern plywood is quite light so extra steps should be taken to ensure the animal does not escape. This can be as basic as adding extra weight to the front of the trap lid but also springs and elastic can be used. A few examples are given here, but remember anything inside the trap needs to be able to withstand being chewed.

On the 'mouse' size this could even be a simple as putting a thick elastic band around the trap.

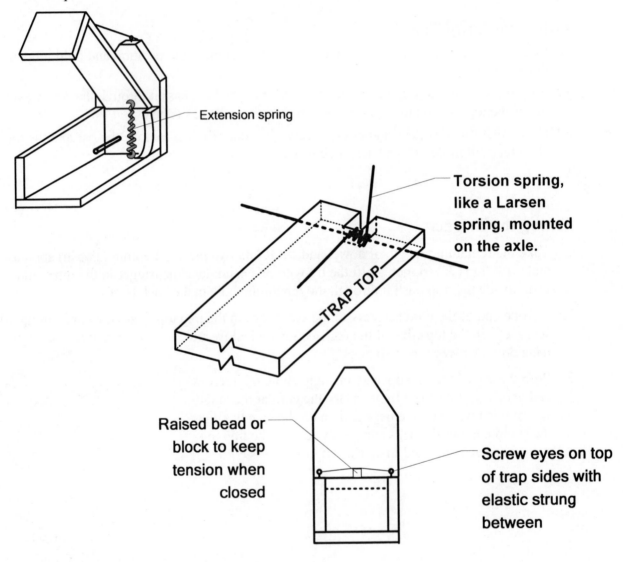

Extension spring

Torsion spring, like a Larsen spring, mounted on the axle.

TRAP TOP

Raised bead or block to keep tension when closed

Screw eyes on top of trap sides with elastic strung between

Chapter 3 - The See-saw Trap

See-saw traps are another type of simple box trap which are effective for rats, squirrels, stoats, mink and even recapturing escaped ferrets. They require no bait but instead use the natural curiosity and the attraction which open ended tunnels have for most small predatory mammals.

The outer box of the trap is basically a tunnel 760mm (30 inches) long with a 100mm (4 inch) internal width. However the height along the sides tapers down which is as a key feature of this trap, as there must be light visible inside end to end. The low end of the tunnel is 125mm (5 inches) high and open, the other end is 180mm (7 inches) high and sealed; but has to let light in, so it can be covered in mesh or Perspex with drilled holes for natural air flow.

The mechanism of the trap is very simple. Inside the box there is a see-saw of thin plywood positioned so that when the trap is set, the end of the see-saw is touching the floor at the tunnel entrance. This creates a gentle ramp but because of the sloping sides the roof and floor look parallel and there is daylight visible down the tunnel.

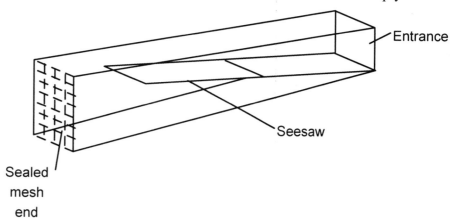

Entrance

Seesaw

Sealed
mesh
end

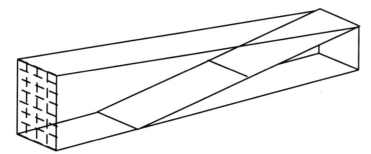

The clearance above the pivot is about 65 – 80mm (2.5 to 3 in) between the surface of the see-saw and the inside of the roof.

Once the animal goes past the pivot point the see-saw tips and the entry 'ramp' rises, touching the roof and closing the box. The lock is a wire 'U' that hangs down from the bottom of the see-saw and prevents it pivoting back.

The Trap In Use

I've had a lot of success putting these in places between cover so that target animals dive into my 'tunnel' as they're scampering across. They also work well positioned on planks or other natural 'bridges' across rivers or ditches. For squirrels the traps can be placed on the ground at the base of trees or high up on garden features like pagodas or walls.

Very wet conditions will affect this trap if the wood swells and the see-saw is unable to move properly.

Flags & indicators

The 'false floor' nature of the see-saw trap can make it quite difficult to spot when it has been triggered, without close inspection. These diagrams illustrate three ideas that have been successfully used to indicate more visibly when a trap is locked.

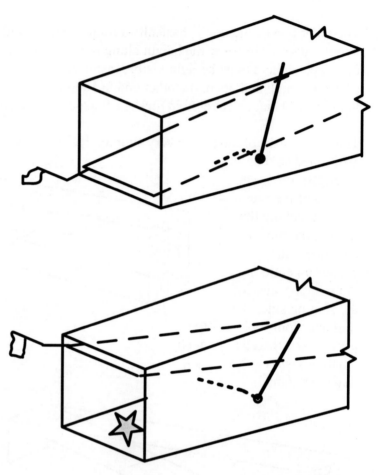

Bright Marker

This simple and very effective method is what I use. Add a high visibility marker to the real floor of the trap at the entrance. Yellow paint, fluorescents stickers or even glued on silver foil would all be suitable but take care not to over do it. A small amount away from the edges will usually be ample and be careful of using anything that leaves a long lasting smell. The disadvantage is that it can only be seen from one side of the trap.

See-saw end flag

Another simple idea uses a thin piece of wire, like a flattened out paper clip. Inserted into a hole in the end of the see-saw this lays on the ground when the trap is set. Once the see-saw is locked the wire is held in the air and any attached flag or wool clearly displayed. The disadvantage of this method is that the thin wire is easily knocked and damaged.

See-saw side flag

The third alternative is the hardest to implement but most professional in appearance and gives 360 degree visibility. A hole is drilled through the side of the box below the see-saw and about halfway between entrance and pivot. A piece heavy gauge galvanised wire is passed through the hole and bent on both sides so as to be at right angles to the portion inside the hole. These two pieces are then twisted away from each other with one piece under the see-saw and the other almost vertical outside the box. Once set up correctly the outside piece (usually slightly longer) will be off balance and trying to swing round on the 'axle' in the box side. The other end will be held down under the see-saw preventing any movement. As the see-saw moves, the inside wire will also be free to move upwards allowing the outside 'flag' to fall. Problems can include sticking in wet conditions and if knocked by wind or animals this flag can act as a lever and close the trap.

A Basic See-saw Trap

A basic see-saw trap is very easy to make but has some practical shortcomings in use. The catch mechanism works well but dealing with the captured quarry becomes difficult.

When you come to inspect the trap, any caught animals will tend to push themselves up the slope of the see-saw away from the mesh opening. In the first place this makes it difficult to see what you have caught and identify it. Secondly it makes humane dispatch awkward unless you transfer the trapped animal to an alternative container.

The Improved Design later in this book was created to address these problems.

Cutting List & Materials

- Outer box pieces and see-saw in 12mm (½ in) exterior grade plywood cut as shown.

- 230mm by 180mm (9" by 7") square of wire mesh; holes no bigger than 12mm (1/2") square.
- 127mm (5") length of 4mm steel rod.
- 220mm (8 ⅝") length of 2.5mm galvanised wire.
- 4 screw eyes (17mm long, 5mm hole diameter)
- 40mm (1.5in) oval nails
- Butt hinge & screws
- 40 mm (1.5in) No 4 bolt & nut & 2 washers
- Wire staples or staple gun.

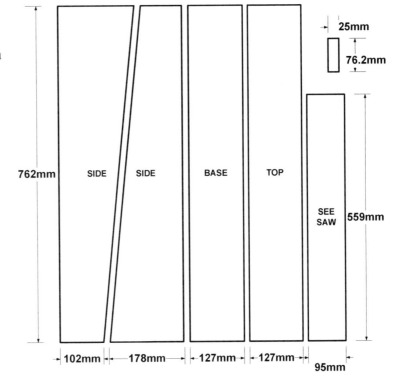

Tools
- Saw
- Hammer
- Drill with 4mm bits
- Screwdriver
- Bradawl
- Vice or pliers.

Optional Tools
Jigsaw or coping saw

Assembly Instructions

Making the Box

1. Take the top and mark lines across at 584mm (23in) and 711mm (28 in) from one end. Cut along these lines to give you three sections.

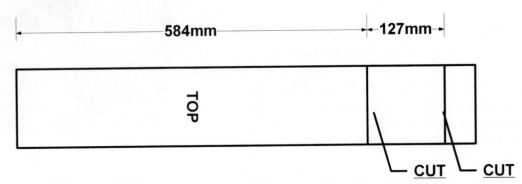

2. Take one of the side pieces; mark a point as shown and drill a 4mm hole. This hole needs to be tight as it will hold the see-saw axle by pushfit.

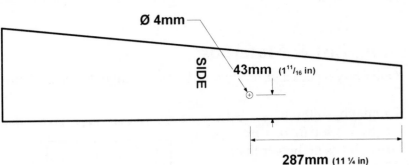

3. Put the two side pieces together and ensure that they are lined up exactly on all edges. Ideally clamp them together in a vice to prevent any movement, then using the first hole as a guide drill through the second piece.

4. Next take the base board and mark a line about 6mm (3/16 in) in from each of the long edges. Take ten nails, (five along each side), and at roughly equal intervals start the nails off along the marked lines.

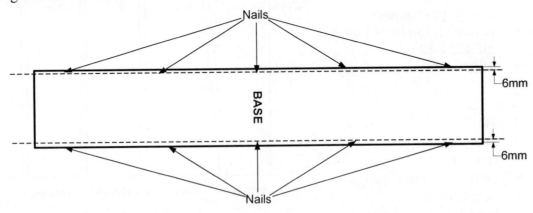

5. Stand the two sides the same way round and with their sloping sides down on the bench and about the right distance apart. Place the base board on top, nails up. Carefully line up one side with the base and hammer in the 5 nails for that side. Then repeat for the other side. Turn over and you should have the basic sloping box shape.

Making and Fitting the See-saw

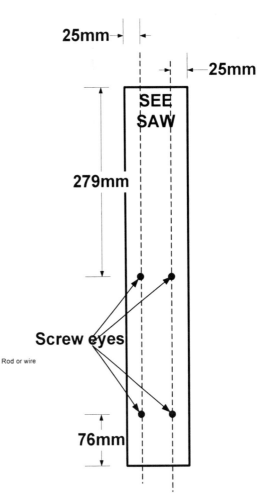

6. Now take the see-saw piece itself and using a bradawl or large nail make four small starter holes; Make two at the centre line 25mm (1 in) in from each side. Make the other two at 76mm (3in) in from one end, also 25mm from the edges.

7. Use these holes to screw in the four screw eyes taking care not to screw the point through to the other side. The eyes should be finished so that the holes are in line in pairs across the width. The middle two will form part of the axle.

8. Bend the screws eyes outwards very slightly – no more than a few millimetres. This helps to reduce any slack between the eyes and the wire and makes the trap close more tightly.

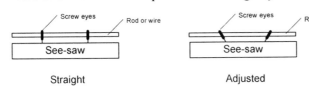

9. Take the 220mm length of galvanised wire and make a bend 84mm (3 ¼ in) from one end. Turn it round and make a bend in the same plane 64mm from the other end. Don't make either bend more than about 30 degrees at this stage and the wire should lie flat.

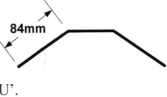

10. Thread the wire through the end pair of screw eyes and squeeze the end of the wire together slightly— but not too much. The ends of the wire should be just inside the edges of the board forming an inverted 'U'.

11. Take the 127mm (5in) length of bar / allthread and push it through one side of the box from the outside. If necessary tap it lightly with a hammer to get it through but be careful not to loosen the sides from the base.

12. Turn the see-saw over so that the screw eyes and galvanised wire are underneath. Swing the wire up towards the end of the board and using you fingers hold it there.

13. Lay the see-saw inside the three sided box. The end with your hand holding the wire should be at the short end of the box and held up at the top of the box. The other end should be allowed to rest on the floor of the box.

14. The 'axle' screw eyes should now be roughly aligned with the axle. Continue to push the axle rod through the side of the box, ensuring that it locates through both screw eyes. Finally tap it home through the hole in the other side. Check that the see-saw moves up and down freely on the axle.

Completing the Trap

15. Take the three pieces of the top and mark lines along the edges as you did in Step 4 for the base. Start the nails; one in each side of the shortest piece, none in the 127mm inch piece and 4 each side of the longest length.

16. Start with the long length of the top and make sure it's flush with the rest of the box at the short end. Hammer the nails in.

17. Swing the see-saw up and down to check that it closes against the underside of the top and that there is clearance under the roof when the see-saw is 'down'.

18. Close the trap and reaching into the box gently squeeze together the end of the galvanised wire 'U' until they touch the floor of the box and prop the see-saw closed. Swing the wire out of the way and reset the trap.

19. Put your hand into the trap and swing the see-saw up and check that it closes and locks correctly. Keep doing this and adjusting the U until it does.

20. Place the middle section (127mm) of the top in position but DO NOT NAIL it. This will become the access hatch.

21. Open the hinge out and lay it flat along the join between the two pieces of the top, with the spindle of the hinge right on the joint. Mark the screw holes on the long piece with pencil then remove the hinge and make starter holes. Replace the hinge and fit the screws in this side.

22. Ensure that the hatch piece is still properly positioned and mark holes for the other side of the hinge. Fit the screws and check that the hatch opens and closes easily.

23. Place the final short length next to the hatch, which should then complete the top of the trap. Ensure there is enough space for the trap door to open freely and then hammer in the nails.

24. Take the remaining piece of plywood, the 76mm x 25mm catch and drill a 4mm hole half an inch from one end. Drill a matching hole through the middle of the small piece of the trap top. Bolt the catch into place with a washer above and below the catch. Check that it pivots freely to open / lock the access hatch.

25. To complete the trap stand it upright on the entrance end. Take the wire mesh rectangle and fold it over the opening—the will be enough wire overhang to on all four sides. Attach it firmly using the wire staples or the staple gun.

Options and Variations.

An alternative door.
Use a solid single piece for the top and replace the mesh end with a hinged panel for access.

The Improved See-saw Trap

I designed the Improved See-saw Trap to make it more practical to use. The dimensions and mechanism are similar to the traditional one, but this design includes a release door and a removable lid with a wire mesh inner.

Cutting List & Materials

- Outer box pieces, door and see-saw in 12mm exterior grade plywood as for Basic See-saw
- Two pieces of wire mesh; holes no bigger than 12mm (1/2 in) square.
  - 100mm by 178mm (4" by 7")
  - 740mm by 178mm (29" by 7")
- 127mm (5") length of 4mm steel rod.
- 220mm (8 $^5/_8$") length of 2.5mm galvanised wire.
- 2 x 105mm (4 $^1/_8$") lengths of roof lath
- 4 screw eyes (17mm long, 5mm hole diameter)
- 1 40mm screw eye
- 1 30mm no6 screw & 2 washers
- 40 mm oval wire nails.

Tools
- Saw
- Hammer
- Drill & 4mm bit
- Screwdriver
- Bradawl
- Vice or pliers.
- Jigsaw or coping saw

Optional Tools
- Router and 15mm bit.

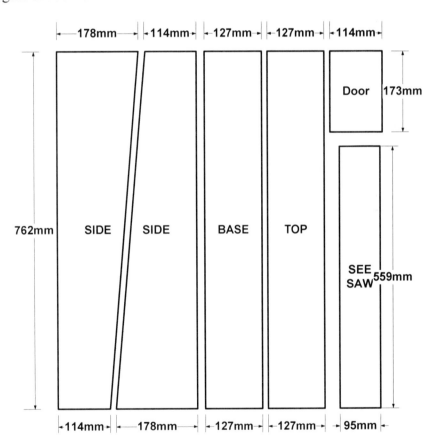

Assembly Instructions

Making the Box

1. Take one of the side pieces; mark a point as shown and drill a 4mm hole. This hole needs to be tight as it will hold the see-saw axle by pushfit.

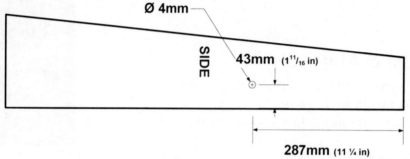

2. Put the two side pieces together and ensure that they are lined up exactly on all edges. Ideally clamp them together in a vice to prevent any movement, then using the first hole as a guide drill through the second piece.

   If you have a router you can make a sliding access door. If you don't, or would rather make a hinged door, ignore steps 3 and 4.

3. Using a router bit of 15mm ($^5/_8$ in) set the fence at approx 12mm (half inch). Set the cut depth to 6mm and on one of the side panels cut a slot from the top sloping edge down to the bottom edge. Set this piece aside.

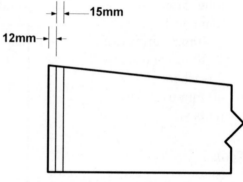

4. Take the other side panel and make a matching cut **on the opposite face**. When complete these slots need to be opposite each other inside the trap.

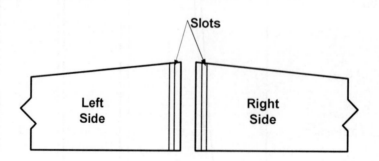

5. Take the base and mark a line about 6mm (3/16") from each of the long edges. Take ten nails, (five along each side), and at roughly equal intervals start the nails off along the marked lines.

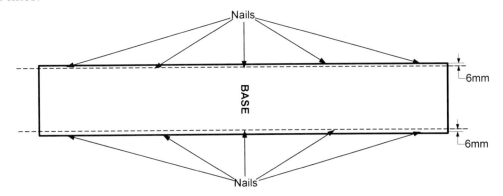

6. Stand the two sides with their sloping sides down on the bench, about the right distance apart and **slots facing each other**. Place the base board on, nails up. Carefully line up one side with the base board; matching outside edges and ends. Hammer in the 5 nails for that side.

7. Repeat for the other side. Turn over and you should have the basic sloping box shape. Check that the routed grove is lined up on opposite sides.

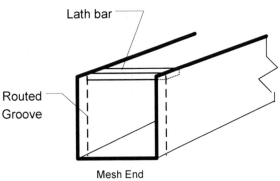

8. Take the two lath pieces and insert them inside the box—holding apart the two top edges. They go in with the wider edge upwards.
The one at the sealed end should be flush with the top edge but just inside the routed groove. (If you're not using a groove for the door then move the lath flush with the end)
Secure with two nails in each end of the lath. If you only use one nail it will twist and not remain in place.

9. The one at the entrance should be flush with the top but must be 60mm in from the end. Position it but **don't nail this one yet.**

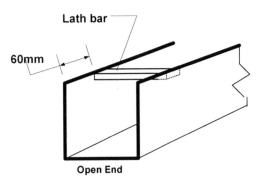

10. Take the plywood door and test slide it into the slot. Trim the door until it moves freely but not too loose.

Making and Fitting the See-saw

11. Now take the see-saw piece itself and using a
bradawl or large nail make four small starter
holes; Make two at the centre line 25mm (1 in)
in from each side. Make the other two at 76mm
(3in) in from one end, also 25mm from the edges.

12. Use these holes to screw in the four screw eyes
taking care not to screw the point through to the
other side. The eyes should be finished so that the
holes are inline in pairs across the width. The
middle two will form part of the axle.

13. Bend the screws eyes outwards very slightly – just
a few millimetres. This helps to reduce any slack
between the eyes and the wire and makes the trap
close more tightly.

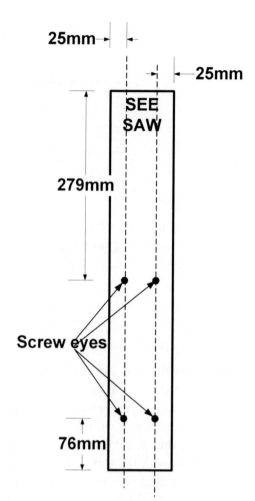

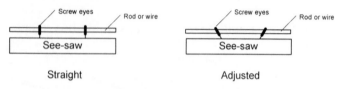

14. Take the 220mm length of galvanised wire and
make a bend 84mm ($3\,^{5}/_{16}$ in) from one end. Turn
it round and make a bend in the same plane 84mm
from the other end. Don't make either bend more
than about 30 degrees at this stage and the wire
should lie flat.

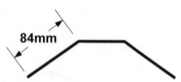

15. Thread the wire through the end pair of screw eyes and
squeeze the end of the wire together slightly— but not too
much. The ends of the wire should be just inside the edges
of the board forming an inverted 'U'.

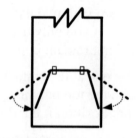

16. Take the 127mm (5in) length of bar / allthread and push it through one side of the box
from the outside. If necessary tap it lightly with a hammer to get it through but be careful
not to loosen the sides from the base.

17. Turn the see-saw over so that the screw eyes and galvanised wire are underneath. Swing
the wire up towards the end of the board and using you fingers hold it there.

18. Lay the see-saw inside the three sided box. The end with your hand holding the wire
should be at the short end of the box and held up at the top of the box. The other end
should be allowed to rest on the floor of the box.

19. The 'axle' screw eyes should now be roughly aligned with the axle. Continue to push the axle rod through the side of the box, ensuring that it locates through both screw eyes. Finally tap it home through the hole in the other side.

20. Check that the see-saw moves up and down freely on the axle.

21. Now check that when the trap is closed and 'locked', the top edge of the see-saw is touching or almost touching the lath spacer positioned at the entrance. Adjust the position of this lath block along the top edge if necessary and nail it in place.

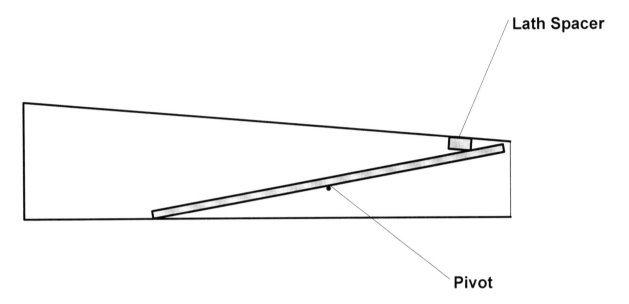

Lath Spacer

Pivot

22. Take the long piece of mesh and lay it over the top of the trap. Ensure that it is does not block the door slot; positioned evenly and fold down the edges. Staple all round and to the lath pieces at the end.

23. Close the trap and reaching into the box gently squeeze together the end of the galvanised wire 'U' until they touch the floor of the box and prop the see-saw closed. Swing the wire out of the way and reset the trap.

24. Put your hand into the trap and swing the see-saw up and check that it closes and locks correctly. Keep doing this and adjusting the U until it does.

Completing the Door

25. Mark a line on one face of the door; all the way round and 20mm (3/4")
    in from the edge. Using a jigsaw or coping saw cut along this line to
    leave a rectangular frame. Lay the remaining mesh piece over this hole
    and secure it to the frame with staples. Slide it down into the slots in the
    trap box and ensure it fits correctly. The door is best fitted with the mesh
    on the inside.

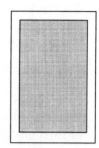

Adding the Top

26. Take the top and lay it in position on the box. Mark with the centre of the two lath pieces.
    At the entrance end drill a single hole in the centre at one of these marks.

27. On the mark at the other end use the drill or router to cut a short slot. This
    needs to run lengthways but is only short; it needs to be just long enough and
    wide enough for the eye of the large screw eye to go through it edgeways.

28. Place the top back in position on the box. With a washer above and below the
    single hole, screw the top down. Don't over tighten as the top needs to pivot
    from side to side.

29. With the top in closed position, mark the
    centre of the 'slot' at the other end. Pivot
    the top to one side and screw the screw eye
    in where you have marked. Rotate the top
    back again and the slot should now drop
    over the head of the screw eye.

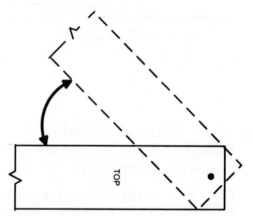

30. To lock the lid turn the eye a quarter turn

31. If you cannot get a screw eye long enough to poke right through the top, use a wire clip
    through the part of the eye that is through.

Options and Variations.

An Alternative Top

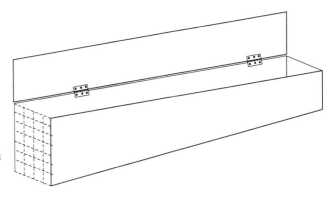

Rather than the pivot method, the top can be hinged using two butt hinges spaced out along the side and the lid locked with a hook and eye. The mesh inner is still required.

Alternative Ends

The sliding wood and mesh door can be replaced with several different alternatives. The three points to remember are that it must let in light, should allow some movement of air and that the width of the routed slot should be adjusted to suit the thickness chosen. At times I have used just heavy gauge mesh on its own. Also Perspex or clear plastic - but not the brittle stuff or it may simply shatter and release the quarry.

Alternative Axle Mounting

Instead of screw eyes to form the axle mountings a more traditional carpentry method can be used. Take a section of roof lath 3.5 inches long (the width of the see-saw) and rout a groove down the middle of one face, 5mm wide by 5mm deep. Mount this block,

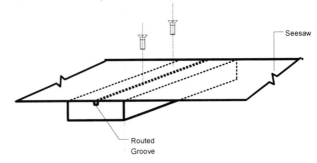

groove upwards, on the underside of the see-saw securing it with short screws, screwed through the see-saw into the block. Ensure that the centre of the groove lines up exactly with the halfway line drawn on the see-saw and is at exactly 90 degrees to the see-saw edge.

See-saw Positioning

At times you might want to vary the length or thickness of the see-saw, or the axle arrangements, or even the length or height of the see-saw box. There can be flexibility in all the areas but the key factor is ensuring the see-saw and axle holes will work. The best way to do this is to 'dry run' where the see-saw will go once the trap is built. Prepare the see-saw first of all, including the axle mountings then take one of the side

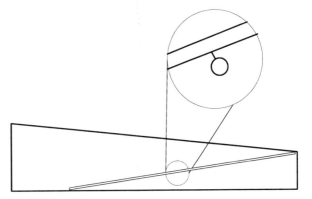

pieces and lay it flat—bottom edge towards you. Then take the see-saw and lay it on top of the side piece — long edge downwards and axle mounting at the bottom. Make sure that one end of the see-saw is right at the top of the low end and that the other is touching the bottom edge of the trap. Sight through the screw eyes / axle mounting and mark the place for the hole on the box side.

Chapter 4 - 'All Mesh' Box Traps

One group of 'all mesh' traps are effectively wire box traps. The main difference in their manufacture is that rather than assembled from lots of separate pieces joined together, most of the trap is usually made from a single large sheet of mesh. The key to a well made mesh trap are the bends in the sheet; getting them straight, right angle and in the right place gives you a stable trap with a natural square section. Get it wrong and the doors won't fit or fall properly, it won't sit flat on the floor and the whole structure will be straining against the ties you use to fix the edges together.

This chapter doesn't give specific details to build any one trap but instead gives guidance on size, shape, materials, technique and a range of doors and triggers so that you can design your own. It will quickly become clear that many of the doors, triggers and techniques covered in this chapter can be transferred to wooden box traps just as well.

Materials

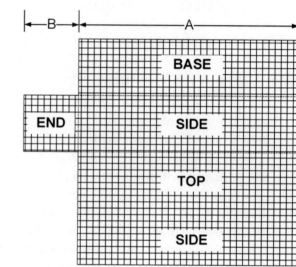

Trap Size & Layout

Ideally the traps should be made from as few pieces as possible - bends are stronger and hold shape better than joins. The diagram shows the typical flat starting piece - the off cuts should be kept to make the door and the treadle.

Dimension, Mesh Size & Gauge.

The mesh needs to have holes small enough to keep things inside but also to stop them firing the trap by reaching for the bait from outside. It also needs to be thick enough to be chew proof; squirrels in particular can gnaw through tougher stuff than you might imagine.

Minimum length in MM (Inches)	A Length	B Width	C Height	Gauge	Max Hole
Squirrel	460mm (18 in)	130mm (5 in)	130mm (5 in)	2mm (14SWG)	12 x12mm (0.5 in)
Rat	255mm (10 in)	130mm (5 in)	130mm (5 in)	2mm (14SWG)	12 x12mm (0.5 in)
Rabbit	760mm (30in)	255mm (10 in)	255mm (10 in)	3mm (10SWG)	90 x 25mm (3.5 x 1in)
Mink	610mm (24in)	180mm (7in)	150mm (6in)	3mm (10SWG)	25 x 25mm (1 x 1 in)
Fox	1830mm (6ft)	760mm (30 in)	915mm (36 in)	4mm (8SWG)	75 x 75mm (3 in)

Shaping The Mesh - The Bending Brake

The trick to bending mesh straight is to have a straight edge to bend it against and be able to keep the mesh in position against it while you apply the pressure to make the bend. In factories they use pneumatic press with a long vice that grips the mesh and forms it around shaped bars, but the same effect can be achieved with a home made wooden brake. Try to use new mesh if you can, it's harder to get a good shape with reclaimed mesh because it is already likely to be bent.

To make the brake you need two matched pieces of hardwood - they need to be at least 12mm (half inch) thick and 80mm (3 inches) wide. The sides and edges need to be perfectly square. If you intend to work with very thick mesh then use larger blocks and consider metal facings to the blocks if you can get them made. The length depends on how wide the mesh sheets are which you expect to be working with - you want the brake to be wider than the mesh. To complete the brake you will need a number of short bolts - just longer than the width of the two blocks together. Drill holes for these first in one block and then, ensuring that the two blocks are perfectly aligned, use them as guides to drill the second set of holes. In one piece countersink the holes so that the ends of the bolts are below the surface of the block - this will form the base so that the brake can lay level and flat when in use. Use a carpenters square to mark lines approximately one inch apart all along the upper face of this block. These lines will be at right angle to the bending face and will be vital in aligning the mesh. Mark similar lines on the top face of the other block.

Using the Brake

Undo the nuts holding the two blocks together and place the base piece flat on the bench, with the bolts sticking upwards. Place the mesh over the bolts and lay it flat on the block - the edge you want to bend 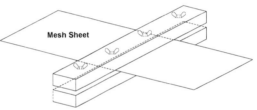 must be exactly along the edge of the bending face. The parallel lines marked on the block with help to get the mesh in position. Carefully replace the top block and loosely do up the nuts. Taking care to keep the mesh in position slowly tighten the nuts until the mesh is firmly held in the brake.

Holding the brake firmly, carefully bend the mesh sheet in the required direction - it sometimes helps to have board to help push on the mesh evenly. Once it is bent to shape use a mallet to hammer it tightly against the bending face. Do this all the way along until you have a tight bend.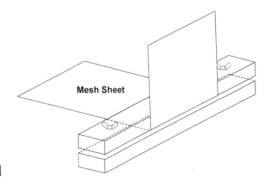

Other Mesh Bending Techniques

There are other ways to bend mesh, particularly small pieces and lighter gauge mesh:

- Two boards held in a vice mimicking the action of the brake.
- 'Mesh bending pliers' - purpose made pliers with lengths of metal plate welded in the jaws to give a wide, straight edge.
- A stout board pushed down onto the mesh on the floor or bench.

Joining the Mesh

The professional way to make joins is using clips which are neat, hardwearing, strong and generally 'chew proof'. If you can get these and are able to use them do so. If you're going to make a lot of traps or cages it's well worth investing in a set of the special crimping pliers. However for the occasional and novice maker plastic cable ties are a good alternative. Cheap, readily available and long lasting, these can be threaded through and pulled tight by hand or with a pair of normal pliers. The one major drawback though is that they are relatively soft and any rat or squirrel could make short work of gnawing through them. The trick here is to do four things:

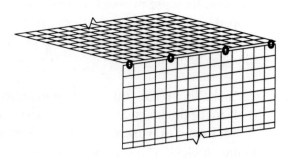

- Try and position them as much as possible away from where the animal will naturally rest in the trap.
- Don't skimp - use more cable ties than you need so that if one or two fail the trap will still hold together.
- Supplement the cable ties with short pieces of wire, wrapped round and twisted. On their own these wire twists would be poor at holding the trap shape square, but after it's fired will help keep the pieces together.
- Carry some spare cable ties when you check your traps

Mounting Swing Doors and Treadles

Doors and treadles can both be mounted simply by creating a loose join of the type described above. Doors should be made from a piece of mesh about the same size as the trap end ("C" by "B"). It should be slightly narrower than 'B' for a swing door, slightly wider for a sliding door and always a little bit longer than C. Treadles should be the same width as the door and about a third of 'C' long. The top edge of the mesh door should be carefully trimmed to that there are no small ends of wire sticking out to snag on the roof. The clips or cable ties need to be adjusted so that the door swings freely but not too much play or the door may move from side to side and catch on the door edges. The best method is to test the door frequently as you tighten the joint.

For the more sophisticated doors an axle arrangement provides a smoother, more reliable hinge and also allows a torsion spring to be included in the design. The axle can be made from dowel, a metal rod or even a small square section length of wood with a nail in each end. It really just depends on the size of the trap which materials you're most comfortable working with.

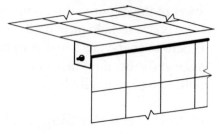

The mountings for the axle can again be wood or metal, mounted on the frame by welding or a simple nut and bolt clamp.

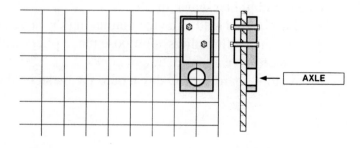

AXLE

Active Doors

Simple 'active' doors that rely on gravity are common and can be very effective, although commercial cage traps will often supplement this by adding a spring. The basic principle remains the same and active doors can be considered in three types:

Sliding or Guillotine Door.

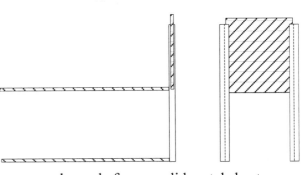

More common on large traps, this door requires a frame around the entrance with grooves or runners for the door to move in. Many permanent fox traps use this type of door and have the runners driven into the ground and the cage built against them. The door itself can be made from mesh but is more commonly made from a solid metal sheet.

Swing outwards

Hinged from the top, the door is set by being swung inwards inside the body of the trap and held against the roof by the trigger. When released it swings back downwards blocking the entrance. Crucially the door is slightly overlong so that it cannot swing through and remains at a slight angle when closed. It is impossible to *push* open from inside and difficult to pull open because the slope of the door means that any animal trying to get out will be stood on the door it is trying to open. Additional security can be added by means of a locking flap; a short strip of mesh hinged to the bottom of the door which then lies flat on the base of the cage. The flap is fitted with short prongs (usually the bent ends of the mesh) which lodge in the mesh of the floor and prevent it being pulled open. Traps using 'swing out' doors need to be a little longer with the trigger set towards the back of the cage to ensure that the animal is not caught under the door when it drops.

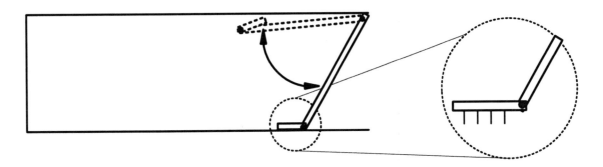

Swing Inwards & lock.

As the name suggests this alternative type of swing door is one that when triggered swings down behind the animal from the outside. This means that the hinge point does not have to be as far into the body of the trap so overall cage length can be shorter. In fact the door is often built so that it actually sticks out a little way when set. The other advantage is that if it does drop early the door is likely to shunt the animal inside. However the potential disadvantage is obvious - any simple door will be easily pushed open again making the trap useless. There are many different locking methods which can be used; such as a sliding peg on the door which drops down and lodges in the mesh floor, or clips of spring steel mounted on the inside of the cage which the falling door forces its way past, and which then spring back. Two of simplest and the most reliable methods are described here.

Drop bar

A rectangular loop of strong wire is hinged separately from the door and swung up in the opposite direction and above the door. When the door drops the end of the wire loop runs down the back of the door until it reaches a 'stop'. The wire is then at roughly a right angle to the door and prevents the door being pushed open.

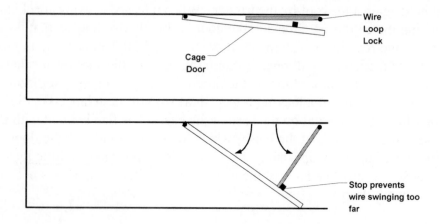

Spring bar

This is a similar principle but this time the locking bar is attached to the bottom of the door and locks by being at right angles to the roof. The key feature here is the spring which pushes the locking bar upright once the door drops. The spring does not need to be very strong as it only moves the bar; it doesn't hold the door closed.

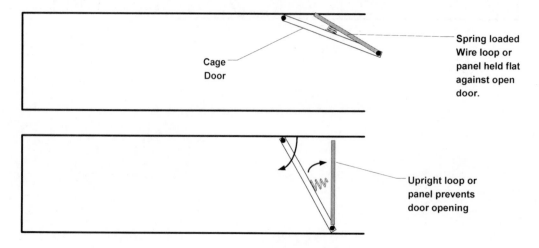

Triggers

The essential companion to an active door is the release mechanism; a pin of some sort which prevents the door from closing until ready and a trigger to pull that pin out of the way at the right time. The two usual types of trigger are the bait pull and the treadle.

Treadle and rod

The simplest type of trigger uses a long straight rod attached to the side of a strip of mesh or metal, which in turn is pivoted on the trap floor as a treadle. To set the trap, the door is swung up and the treadle tilted so that the end of the rod slides through the door and the roof of the trap together. Poked through both meshes like this the rod keeps the door open. Bait is put at the back of the trap, well behind the treadle and not under it. Any animal trying to reach the bait will push or tread on the treadle, which will pivot down, pulling the rod and releasing the door. In practice it is usually necessary to trim some of the mesh squares to create an elongated rectangle in the door so that the rod can fall away cleanly.

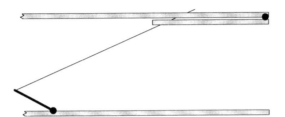

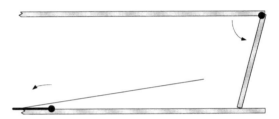

Variations of this, where the rod does not go through the door itself, are suitable for the more complex doors. One option is to have a loop of wire or cross bar near the top of the trap; the rod passes over this bar and just tucks under the end of the door.

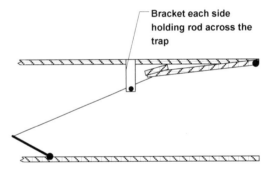

Bracket each side holding rod across the trap

Another option is to have the rod running on the outside of the trap connected to a simple linkage. The bottom of this linkage is bent inside the trap latched under the door. When the treadle is pressed, the rod rotates the linkage and the latch moves out from under the door, releasing it.

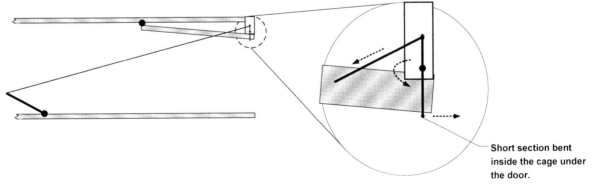

Short section bent inside the cage under the door.

The final variation is to have short rod going straight up and just passing through the trap roof. A ring fits over this rod attached to a cord holding the door in set position. When the treadle is pressed, the rod pulls through the roof, the ring slips off and the cord is released. This design can be used for a double entry trap by having two doors / rings hooked on the same rod.

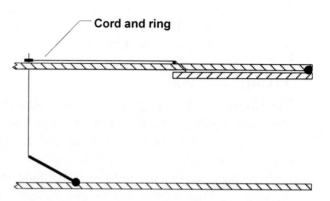
Cord and ring

Bait Pull and Peg

This trigger relies on the target animal reaching the bait and trying to remove it. It's particularly suitable for large predators like fox, mink and even rats but not so good for mice which, not being strong enough to pull the bait, will nibble it where it is.

This simple mechanism uses a bar pivoted through the roof of the trap, with the inside portion much longer to give maximum leverage from the animals 'pull'. This is particularly important for traps using heavy metal sliding doors where there is a lot of pressure on the release pin making it hard to pull out.

The bait needs to be securely attached so as not to come away too easily and the bar needs to be strong enough not to bend.

To use this trigger with swing doors you will need a loop attached to the door and poking up through the roof of the trap.

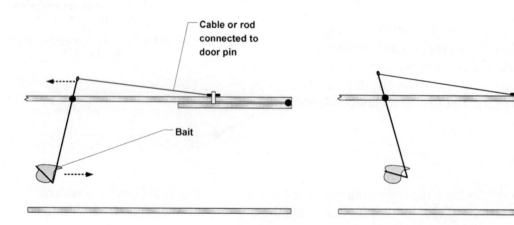
Cable or rod connected to door pin

Bait

For sliding doors the peg fits into a hole in the door itself and only requires a firm surface on the trap roof to rest against.

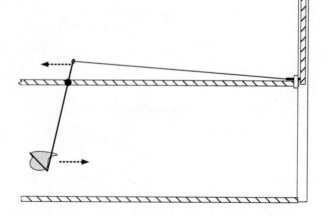

Passive Doors

I've used the term 'Passive Doors' to describe entrances which aren't set and then sprung in the way discussed so far. Some of these doors require a bit more effort by the animal and some may not be as secure as an active door. However they do enable you make 'multi-catch' traps because there is no difference between when the trap is first set and after it has caught.

Push Past

The door in this case is made from vertical loops of wire attached to an axle mounted across the trap at roof height. The wires need to be strong but light weight and fixed to the axle so that they all move together as a single door, not as individual wires. This can be done by welding the wires to a metal axle or pushing them into holes drilled in a wooden dowel. These wires need to be close enough together to prevent escape.

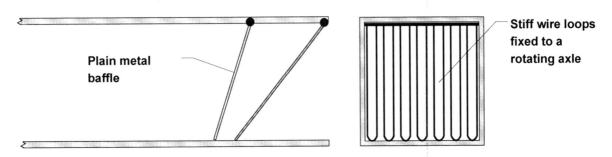

Plain metal baffle

Stiff wire loops fixed to a rotating axle

If sufficiently attracted by the bait, an animal will push its way inside the trap raising the door as it goes. As the animal passes through, the door drops back down again behaving just like the Swing Outwards door described earlier. Any other animals approaching the trap will be attracted by both the bait and the previous catch and process repeats.

Because the door doesn't change after a catch, we can't use any of the locking mechanisms discussed so far. Instead the reliability of this door can be improved by fitting a full width baffle as a sort of inner door. Hung on a separate axle further inside the trap, this baffle of sheet metal will be raised up out of the way when the quarry pushes its way under the main door. The baffle then falls back to cover the real door on the inside and so any efforts to escape is wasted on this and not on the external door. This diagram illustrates the passage of an animal through the double doors.

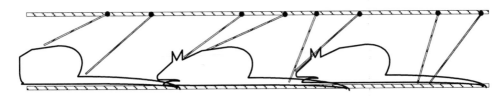

It is easy to see how this type of door can be used at either end to make a double entry, multi-

catch trap. Furthermore it can be used in combination with any of the Active Doors so that the first catch is made easily in an 'open' trap but adding the multi-catch capability.

Another type of baffle is a simple vertical strip across the floor with a vertical edge about 15mm high. This stops the edge of the door from being pulled up by clawing. Make sure it's far enough back to allow the door to *just* open.

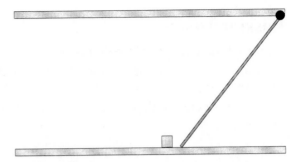

You can use this type of baffle on the see-saw traps – particularly if the see-saw isn't closing firmly against the box floor.

Funnel

The 'funnel' is very widely used in traps of all kinds; who hasn't seen a lobster pot? The principle is that the quarry animal will squeeze inside, aided by the shape of the funnel and lured by the bait. Once inside it is unable to escape either because it cannot find the small exit hole or because it cannot get through it. Funnels are not very effective for ground vermin but work well for birds both horizontally and vertically.

This example works well for magpies. Fitted in the side of any large mesh cage – at least 600mm (23 ½ in) wide and tall, 1200mm (47in) deep to allow clearance out of the funnel.

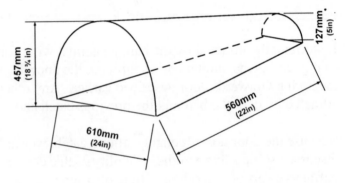

Chapter 8 covers some other variations on the funnel principle.

Chapter 5 - The Rabbit Drop Box

The rabbit drop box is a large scale, permanent set, multi-catch trap. It consists of a fairly deep pit with a pivoted trapdoor above it and a tunnel to channel the rabbits over the trapdoor. The trapdoor falls away under the weight of a passing rabbit, dropping it into the pit or 'box'. With the rabbit no longer on it, the door is free to swing back to reset the trap. Placed across a fence line this trap creates an artificial route that rabbits will begin to use regularly—at which point the trap can be 'switched on' and will take a large number of rabbits very

quickly. It takes a bit of setting up but once in place will work reliably over a long period. For best results the trap should be installed at the same time that rabbit proof fencing is erected. If added to an existing fence line, allow the trap to settle in and then slowly block off all the other gaps that the rabbits use.

The tunnel should be orientated so that it is almost parallel to the fence line, because rabbits will run along the fence line looking for a way through. The trap can be used with the tunnel at right angles to the fence but it less effective. One end of the tunnel must be flush with the fence and the bulk of the trap on the side the rabbits are going to, not coming from.

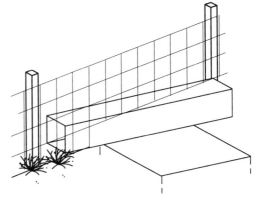

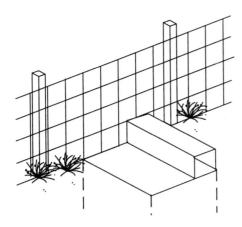

You might question why a trap like this would be needed if a fence has been installed. In practice few fences are truly rabbit proof so you're better to establish and control the rabbit routes. Rabbits have been known to climb fences.

The detailed design I have provided here is for an asymmetrical trapdoor which uses the weight of one wider side to swing the door closed. Once you understand the principle of the structure the trap can be improved by using a narrower but weighted counter balance or even installing a spring. Commercial Drop Boxes are made of galvanised steel and use a lightly sprung door.

Cutting List & Materials

- Lengths of 35mm x18mm roof lath in lengths as below:
  - 5 Frame Rails   @ 710mm (28 in)
  - 2 Cross Rails   @ 670mm (26 $^3/_8$ in)

- 12mm <u>marine</u> grade plywood in sizes as below:
  - Trap Door   @460mm by 660mm   (18$^1/_8$ in by 26 in)
  - Access Hatch   @205mm by 670mm   (8$^1/_{16}$ in by 26$^3/_8$ in)
  - Tunnel Roof   @220mm by 1070mm   (8$^5/_8$ in by 42½ in)
  - 1 Low Tunnel Side   @180mm by 1070mm   (7$^1/_8$ in by 42 in)
  - 1 Tall Tunnel Side   @250mm by 1070mm   (10$^{13}/_{16}$ in by 42 in)
  - 2 Short Housing Rails @710mm by 70mm   (28 in by 2 ¾ in)
  - 1 Long Housing Rail @734mm by 70mm   (29 in by 2 ¾ in)
  - 4 Box Sides   @690mm by 610mm   (27$^1/_8$ in by 24 in)

- 690mm (27$^1/_8$) length of 6mm steel allthread
- 4 40mm Turn Buttons
- no 6 Screws 40mm (1½ in) long
- 4 washers 6mm internal diameter.
- 40mm galvanised nails (Use these throughout unless otherwise stated).
- 30mm oval wire nails.
- 2 small screw eyes and a length of light, rot proof cord.

Optional
- Weld mesh box floor   710mm by 710mm   (28 in by 28 in)

A bit more on materials

With this trap there is a bit more discussion needed on materials than on previous traps. First off this trap is going to be sunk into a hole in the ground so will spend a lot of time fairly damp or even wet. It is essential that all the parts of the trap are thoroughly treated with a good quality wood preservative – a low odour variety such as Cuprinol but avoid creosote as the smell will act as a deterrent for months or even years.

In these plans the Holding Box is made from plywood and is open at the bottom. If you are working in sandy soil or find that successive catches are beginning to burrow out, wire mesh can be attached across the bottom of the box to create a free draining floor. Clearly it's much easier to do that before you install the trap.

Another option is to make the entire Holding Box from heavy duty galvanised weld mesh – base and four sides. It needs to be strong enough to support the trap frame and unlike the plywood is likely to last better in the damp conditions. A mesh Box will have thinner walls so aim to make it the outside dimensions of the plywood one. One word of caution though is that 50mm (2in) weld mesh can provide the rabbits with a very convenient ladder up the side of the pit and with the basic design it is quite realistic for them to push the back of the trap door up and escape. So if you want to use mesh you're better using one of the variations discussed at the end.

Assembly Instructions

Making the Trap Door

1. Take one of the 710mm Frame Rails and use the marking gauge to make a line all the way along the centre of one of the wide faces.

2. Mark a line 25mm in from one end and using a carpenter's square mark it all the way around. Do the same at the other end. Check the distance between the two lines is 660mm (26 in).

3. Using the router cut a slot along the centre line. The slot needs to be 6mm wide by 6mm deep ($^1/_4$ inch). You would find that it is very difficult to keep the slot straight when you get to the very ends of the rail because there is nothing for the router fence to slide along. Don't worry, the timber has been left deliberately overlong to allow for this and we're going to trim the ends off. Just make sure the slot runs as far as the lines marked at each end.

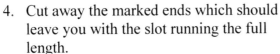
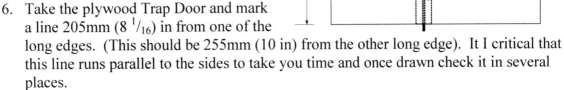

4. Cut away the marked ends which should leave you with the slot running the full length.

5. Place the 690mm length of allthread into the slot and leave the rail slot upwards on the bench.

6. Take the plywood Trap Door and mark a line 205mm (8 $^1/_{16}$) in from one of the long edges. (This should be 255mm (10 in) from the other long edge). It I critical that this line runs parallel to the sides to take you time and once drawn check it in several places.

7. Mark four points at approximately 10mm each side of this line, spread out down the length – don't put them in opposite pairs. Drill 3mm holes at these points and countersink them.

8. Place the trap door on top of the rail and allthread. The ends of the allthread must be perfectly in line with the line on the Trap Door. Carefully screw the two pieces together through the 8 holes.

9. Check that the allthread axle and the line are still aligned.

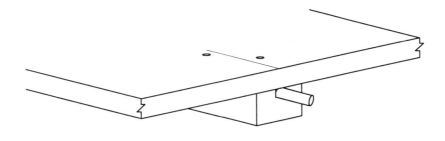

Preparing the Top Frame

10. Take the four remaining 710mm Frame Rails

11. Use the marking gauge to make a line along the <u>centre</u> of the wide face at one end. Turn the rail over and at the same end score a matching line on the other side. Be sure to use the gauge from the same edge each time so that the lines are perfectly opposite.

12. Measure in from the end of the rail 19mm (the thickness of the lath) and using a carpenter's square mark from the centre line out to one edge. Use the square to continue this line onto the edge and across the opposite face until it meets the other scored line.

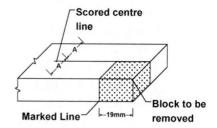

13. Use the square again to join the two scored lines across the very end of the rail and you will have marked a block on the corner of the rail. Shade this with the pencil to indicate which side will be removed.

14. Using two saw cuts, remove this block.

15. Drill a 2mm pilot hole from the wide face through the shoulder you have just made.

16. Turn the rail round and repeat at the other end, ensuring that <u>both removed blocks are on the same edge</u>.

17. Repeat for steps 10 to 15 for all four Frame Rails.

18. Take just 2 of the rails and lay them flat on the bench, cut-outs facing each other. (See diagram below)

19. Measure 228mm (9 in) along from the very end of the Rail, (<u>not from the cut out</u>) and mark a point 15mm ($^9/_{16}$ in) down from the top edge. Drill a 6mm hole at this point but only about halfway through the rail - NOT right through. This will form the housings for the trap door axles. (If you do drill through by accident, you can use allthread a little longer at 800mm (31½ in) so that you can fix nuts on the outside)

20. Measure 486mm (19 $^1/_8$ in) from the same start point. Mark a line and drill two 3mm pilot holes, 10mm ($^3/_8$ in) either side of the mark and 10mm up from the shouldered edge.

21. Measure 40mm (1 $^9/_{16}$ in) from the opposite end. Mark a line and drill two 3mm pilot holes, 10mm either side of the mark and 10mm up from the shouldered edge.

22. Repeat this for the second rail but because the rail is the other way up, the holes should be 'opposite' as shown.

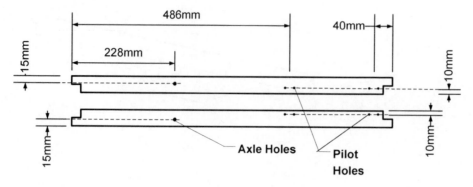

Assembling the top Frame

23. Take the trapdoor you prepared in step 8 and position it between the two drilled Frame Rails with the axle opposite the holes; plywood upwards and the short side towards the short end of the rail.

24. Lay the other Frame Rails in position to complete the ends of the square.

25. Start nails in all the 3mm pilot holes.

26. Locate one of the Frame rails into the end of one of the Drilled Rails. The sections you removed fit together to form a halving joint. (Fig A). Check that the pieces are flush and square - drive in the nails to fix this corner.

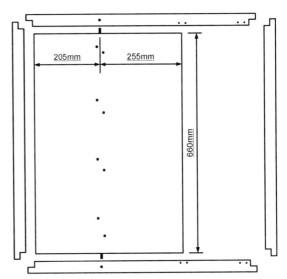

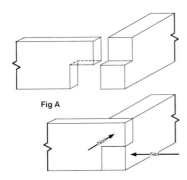

Fig A

27. Fix the other Frame Rail to the other end of the same Drilled Rail to give you three sides of a square.

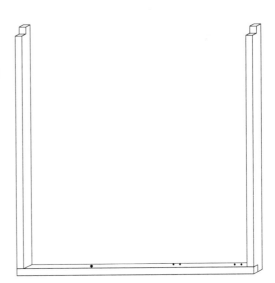

28. Place two washers on each end of the allthread. Locate the axle into the corresponding hole on the attached Drilled Rail. Push on firmly but not too tight.

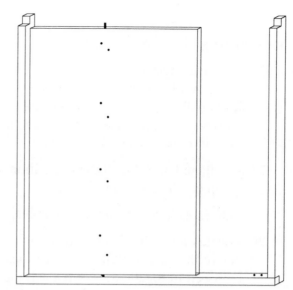

29. Position the remaining Drilled Rail – locating it on the end of the axle and into the halving joint at each end. If the halving joints won't fit then shorten the allthread slightly. Check it is square all round and nail the joints in place.

30. Lift the frame off the bench and the trapdoor should pivot freely, just clearing the frame edge on one side. The piece on the inside, being slightly larger, will naturally swing down.

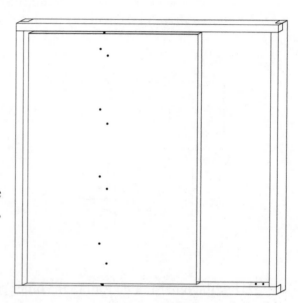

31. Turn the whole thing over and lay it on a flat level surface, trapdoor downwards. The trap door should be flush with the frame rails on the bench and so should not rock about.

32. Take one Cross Rail and place it across the frame level with the middle sets of pilot holes. It should be wide side down, parallel to the axle of the trap and a little over the back edge of the trapdoor itself. It will also be slightly below the rim of the frame.

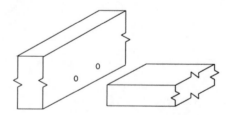

33. Position this carefully and drive nails through the pilot holes. Turn the frame back over and the rail you just fitted should be acting as a 'swing stop' to prevent the door swinging right round. Press the front edge down a little and release – the door should swing back to level with the top edge of the frame.

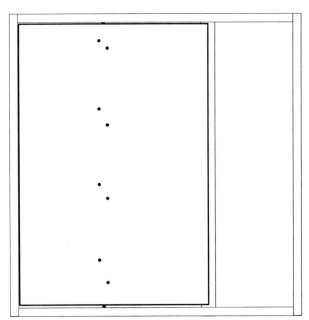

Viewed from top with Trap Door & Swing Stop fitted.

34. Take the Access Hatch and lay it in the space left in the frame. One edge will rest on the cross piece you've just fitted, the other edge with fall through. Holding it carefully in place, turn the frame back upside down again.

35. The Access Hatch should now be lying on the bench, inside the frame. Slide it backwards away from the Trap Door until it is right against the back Rail. Place the remaining Cross Rail on top of the Access Hatch and slide it back until it is also right against the back Rail; the ends should be in inline with the remaining pilot holes. Check that everything is flush and drive in nails through the pilot holes.

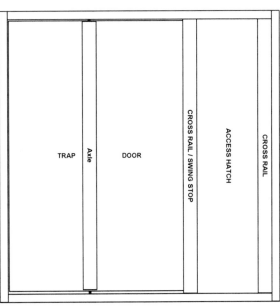

View from Underside – all rails and panels fitted

36. Turn the frame back a final time and check the Access Hatch is still slid to the back. Check that the Trap Door still swings freely.

Fitting the Box Housing

The Box Housing is an outer plywood frame designed to create a 'lip' for the holding box to fit into.

37. Take the three Housing Rails and mark three points all 17mm ($^{10}/_{16}$ in) from one long edge. Mark one 100mm ($3^{15}/_{16}$ in) in from each end plus one in the centre. Drill 3mm holes at these points and counter sink them.

38. Bring back the completed frame top, remove the Access Hatch and put it to one side. Lay the frame on a large flat surface top down (i.e. with the axle visible.)

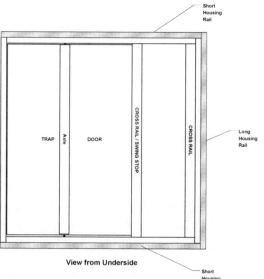

39. Take one of the Short Housing Rails and place it with the drilled holes down, against the side, outside edge of the frame. The ends should be flush with the ends of the frame. Secure with three screws through the drilled holes and into the frame Rail.

40. Fit the other Short Housing Rail to match on the opposite side.

41. Take the Long Housing Rails and place it holes down most against the back, outside edge of the frame (i.e. the rail furthest from the axle.) The end should overlap the Short Housing Rails you've just fitted and be flush with the outer edges. Secure with three screws through the drilled holes and into the frame Rail.

Making the Tunnel

42. Take the three pieces of the tunnel. Along each edge of the tunnel roof section mark a line 6mm ($^1/_4$ in) in from the edge. Start nails off along these lines, roughly 100mm (4 in) apart.

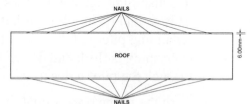

43. Take the Tall Side and along one long edge mark two sections; these should be one in each corner, 168mm ($6^5/_8$ in) long and 35mm ($1^3/_8$ in) wide. Using the saw carefully remove these pieces and discard them. Drill 3 mm holes along the remaining piece; 53mm (2 in) up from the edge and evenly spaced.

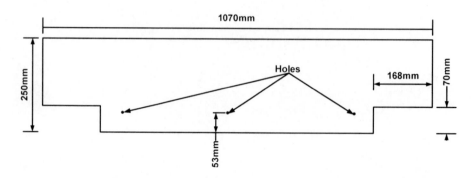

44. Take the Low Side, stand it upright on the bench and line it up vertically under one row of nails. Check that it's flush all the way around and drive in the nails.

45. Stand the Tall Side vertically on the bench with the drilled holes at the bottom and position the Roof over the top edge. Check that it's flush all the way around and drive in the nails. The resulting tunnel will be 'lopsided' with one side longer than the other – this is quite correct.

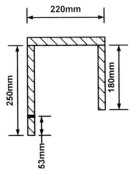

Finishing off the Top

46. Bring back the completed frame top and lay it on the bench the right way up and with the front towards you (i.e. the side without a plywood housing).

47. Place the tunnel across the front of the frame, tall edge towards you. The tunnel should sit level on the frame with the tall edge touching the bench. Check that the shoulders cut out of the tall side are flush with the frame and secure the tunnel with screws through the drilled holes.

48. Reposition the Access panel onto the frame and screw a Turn Button onto the frame either side. These will twist to lock or release the hatch.

49. Screw the other two turn buttons further along the frame so that they can lock the Trap Door closed when necessary.

50. Drill a hole through the middle of the access panel to act as a handle to remove it. Either a 30mm diameter hole so that you can push a finger through to lift it or use a smaller hole with a length of knotted string through.

51. Open the trapdoor and insert a screw eye into the underside, near the edge and roughly in the middle. Insert the second screw eye into the side of the swingstop. Make it almost in line but not quite or else they will clash and stop the door closing.

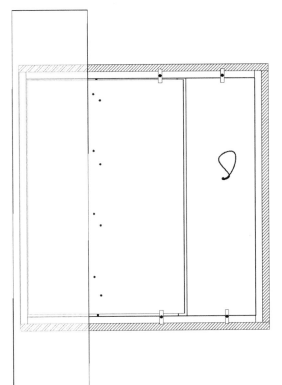

Making the Holding Box

52. The holding box sits underneath the frame for the rabbits to fall into and be retained. Take the one plywood Box Side and mark a line down one of the 610mm sides, 10mm in from the edge. Start nails off along this line

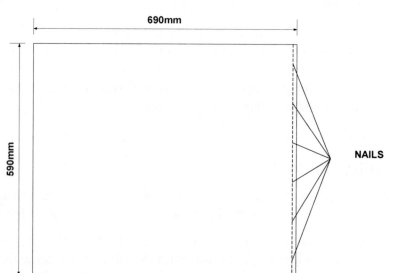

53. Repeat for the other three sides.

54. Place one side vertically on the bench, nails facing you and towards the bottom. Place another side horizontally on top, nails upwards and towards you. Line the edge and ends up and hammer in the nails to join the two sides.

55. Rotate it round so that the first piece is flat on the bench and the piece you nailed is now vertical.

56. Place another side horizontally on top, nails upwards and towards you. Line the edge and ends up and hammer in the nails to join the two sides.

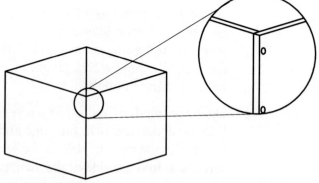

57. Rotate again and repeat to add the fourth side.

58. Rotate one more time to hammer in the final nails.

59. If you've decided to use the mesh floor, attach that over one end using a staple gun or wire staples.

Final Checks & Adjustments

60. Place the box on the bench or floor, mesh side down.

61. Place the trap top on top of the box – the edges of the box should locate inside the plywood Housing Rails all the way round.

62. Undo the trap door turn buttons, put your hand inside the tunnel check that the trap door opens and closes freely. You can add weight to the trap door to alter the sensitivity; the further from the axle the more leverage and effect the weight has.

63. Prop the trap door open and tie the cord between the two screw eyes. Shorten the length so that this 'check cord' prevents the door opening too far. Once this is fitted the trapdoor should always swing back closed.

Options and Variations

The Narrow, Weighted Door

The design above relies on the weight of the wider side of the trapdoor to close and reset the door. A simple development is to reduce the overall width of the trap door down to 305mm (12 in); 205mm trap side and 100mm counterweight. The advantage of this design is that it reduces the scope for rabbits to escape through the back of the door and it increases the access area when trying to get the rabbits out.

In order to make it work you will need to add weight to the counterweight side – typically lead but you could use any heavy substance. The heavier it is the less you need and attaching it further from the pivot increases the leverage.

Structurally you will also need to make a few small alterations. The Access Panel will need to be bigger to take up the space created by the reduced Trap Door – make it 360mm by 670mm. You will need to adjust the position of the Swing Stop when drilling the pilot holes in step 19; instead of 486mm you need to measure 331mm. Also reposition the turn buttons.

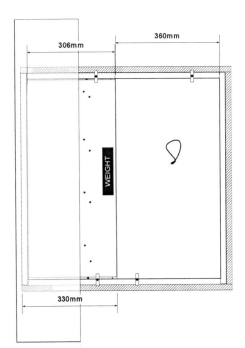

In practice you can vary the width of the door to suit yourself provided you make the same corresponding adjustments.

The Sprung Door

An alternative to this weight is to add a spring to act as the door return, in one of two ways.

The simplest is to use an expansion spring which are commonly available in DIY shops. Attach one of these to the bottom of the narrow counter balance section and the side of the frame. For best results attach one each side to get an even return. The problem with this arrangement is positioning the spring so that it can stretch far enough for the door to open and remain under tension enough to hold it in the down position.

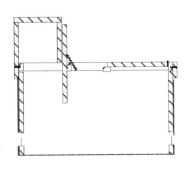

The better solution is to use a radial torsion spring as the Larsen trap does, but not one as strong. This would slide over the axle at one end with one spring arm attached to the trap door and the other braced against the frame rails. This requires a bit more skill to fit; it involves shortening the routed axle bar a little and cutting a section out of the trap door.

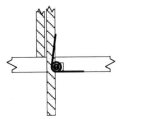

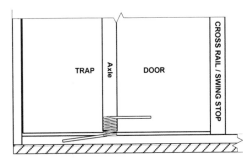

Using the Trap

One you have installed the trap, it's best to leave it for a week or so with the trap door locked. Allow the rabbits to get used to using it regularly and inspect the fence for signs of any other holes that they're using. Gradually block these off.

Once there is established traffic through the tunnel, switch the turn buttons to release the door and inspect the trap daily. To get the rabbits out, lock the trap door then undo the other turn buttons to release the access panel. Reach in and grab the rabbits one at a time and kill them by breaking the neck. There are several methods for doing this and you should ensure that you can do it quickly and humanely. There is lots of guidance in ferreting books and websites.

Remember the pit is quite deep and you may have to lie down to reach the back corners. If you are not used to handling rabbits you may want to wear gardening gloves as they have sharp nails, teeth and a powerful kick.

To increase the access to the drop box you can undo the 'check cord' and prop the trap door open. You can also adjust the length of this cord if the trap is not positioned level and is not closing properly.

Rabbits provide a good quality, free range, healthy meat and are suitable for human and animal consumption.

Chapter 6 – The Larsen Trap

The Larsen trap is mainly a trap for magpies, although it also has been known to catch crows, jays and other corvids. It is one of the few traps where it is legal to use a live bird to catch others - not as 'bait' in the usual sense but by using the natural instinct of these birds to guard their territory. Dominant birds, or new birds entering an area, will approach the call bird and in the course of the encounter will be caught.

The trap itself is divided into two halves; one forming the permanent cage for the 'call bird' and the other half divided into two catch chambers. Each catch chamber has a pivoted door which is sprung and folds down inside the trap when it is set. A pair of dowels are then placed end on end between the door and the inner wall, held in position by the tension of the sprung door. When a bird lands on this 'split perch' while trying to get to the call bird, the perch will collapse—dropping the bird into the catch chamber and releasing the lid to spring shut.

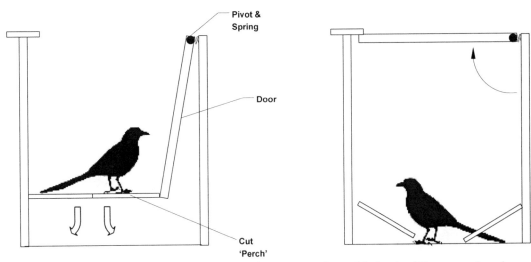

The law which allows the use of live decoys in this way carries with it significant and serious responsibilities - by law you must not cause unnecessary suffering to the call bird. In practical terms this means:

- <u>Daily</u> checks to monitor the health of the call bird, to providing food and water and to remove any caught birds.
- A trap big enough for the call bird to spread its wings.
- To provide shelter. The trap has a covered section but in very bad weather more may be required, particularly on the sides.
- Any injured call bird must be dispatched quickly and humanely. It is good practice to replace the call bird regularly.
- NOTE: In Scotland Larsen traps must now be registered and be labelled with a unique identification number.

Cutting List & Materials

- Lengths of 35mm x18mm roof lath in lengths as below:
    - 4 long rails   @ 813mm (32 inches)
    - 4 short rails   @ 775mm (30.5 inches)
    - 4 cross rails   @ 775mm (30.5 inches)
    - 5 short uprights   @ 438mm (17.25 inches)
    - 4 long uprights   @ 474mm (18 $^{11}/_{16}$ inches)
    - 4 trap door sides   @ 330mm (13 inches)
    - 4 trap door ends   @ 290mm (11 $^{7}/_{16}$ inches)
    - 2 access sliders   @ 356mm (14 inches)

- 6 or 9mm exterior grade plywood in sizes as below:
    - Cover   405mm (16 in) square
    - Access hatch   190mm (7.5 in) square
    - Divider   510mm by 380mm (20 in by 15 in)
    - Swing stop   405mm by 125mm (16 in by 5 in)

- Sections of wire mesh
    - 2 x doors   320mm (12 ½ in) square
    - Roof section   405mm (16 in) square
    - Divider   812mm by 510mm (32 in by 20 in)
    - 4 x Sides   812mm by 510mm (32 in by 20 in)
    - Base   812mm (32in) square

- Matched pairs of springs
- 1m length of 6mm steel allthread
- 8mm Dowel
    - 2 fixed perches of length 546mm (21.5 inches)
    - 2 x lengths of 178mm (7 inch)
    - 2 x lengths of 159mm (6 $^{1}/_{4}$ inches)
- Pack of 40mm galvanised nails (Use these through out unless otherwise stated).
- 22 x Size 6 screws 25mm (1 in) long
- 2 x large nails 65mm (2 ½ in) long
- 8 Corrugated Fasteners (13mm)
- 4 Small fence wire staples

Tools

- Saw
- Hammer
- Marking gauge
- Chisel & mallet
- Drill with 2 mm, 3mm and 6mm bit
- Screwdriver
- Bradawl
- Jigsaw or coping saw
- Staple gun and staples

Preparing the Parts

Preparing the Rails

1   Take the one of the Long Rails and use the marking gauge to make a line along the <u>centre</u> of the wide face at one end. Turn the rail over and at the same end score a matching line on the other side. Be sure to use the gauge from the same edge each time so that the lines are perfectly opposite.

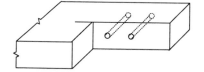

2   Measure in from the end of the rail 35mm (the width of the lath) and using a carpenter's square mark from the centre line out to one edge. Use the square to continue this line onto the edge and across the opposite face until it meets the other scored line.

3   Use the square again to join the two scored lines across the very end of the rail and you will have marked a block on the corner of the rail. Shade this with the pencil to indicate which side will be removed.

4   Using two saw cuts, remove this block.

5   Drill two 2mm pilot holes from the top through the shoulder you have just made. Keep them away from the rail end as other holes will be needed here.

6   Turn the rail round and repeat at the other end, ensuring that <u>both removed blocks are on the same edge</u>.

7   Now measure the midpoint of the rail length and using the square mark it round on all four sides.

8   Repeat steps 1 to 7 for all four Long Rails.

Assembling the frame ends.

9   Bring together two of the Long Rails, 2 Long Uprights and 1 Short Upright.

10 Start a nail in one of the pilot holes at each end of each rail.

11 Place the Long Upright vertical on the bench. Taking a Rail, fit the end of the upright into the housing you made in the end of the Rail.   It should fit neatly in, with the end of the Upright in contact with the pilot holes. Keeping the pieces as tight as you can, drive in the nail.

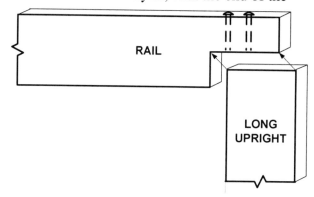

12 Turn the rail around and fit the other Long Upright into the other end and drive in the nail.

13 Flip the structure over so that the first Rail is now on the bench and the Uprights are sticking up in the air. Locate the second Long Rail onto the uprights in the same way and drive in the nails.

14 You should now have a firm rectangular frame.

15 Go back round all four corners and drive nails into the four remaining pilot holes at these joints. (Not the holes in the centre of the rail).

16 Lay the frame flat on the bench and position the Short Upright between the top and bottom Rails. It should be flush with the rails on both side and centred on the centre lines you marked earlier.

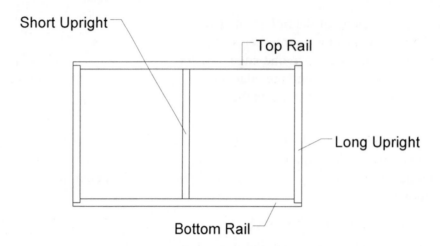

17 Secure it by hammering a corrugated fastener across the join at each end. A staple is used to reduce the number of nails going though the Rail at this point. It will hold the upright in place but won't be a very firm joint - strength will be added when the wire mesh covering is stapled into place.

18 Using the 2mm bit, drill vertical pairs of pilot holes in the top and bottom rail along the centre line immediately above / below the Short Upright you've just put in place.

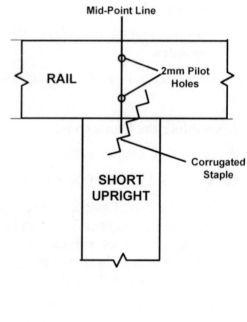

19 Using the same 2mm bit, drill pairs of pilot holes at each corner about 9mm ($^1/_4$ in) in from the end of the top and bottom rails.

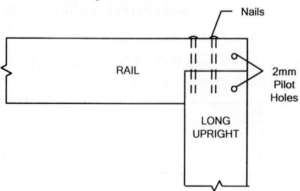

20 Repeat steps 9 to 19 to make a second end frame.

Preparing the Cross Pieces - halving joints

21 Take the four of the Cross Rails and lay the side by side on the bench. Mark the midpoint of the length on all of them and check they line up. Then using a carpenters square mark this centre line all round on all 4 rails.

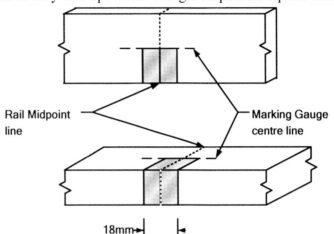

Rail Midpoint line

Marking Gauge centre line

18mm

22 Using the marking gauge again, make a short line along the <u>centre</u> of the wide face, crossing where you've marked the midpoint. Turn the rail over and score a matching line on the other side. Be sure to use the gauge from the same edge each time so that the lines are perfectly opposite.

23 Measure 9mm either side of the midpoint line and using the square mark lines between the centre line and one edge. Use the square to continue the lines round the rail until you meet the centre line on the other side. You will end up with a square section marked on one edge and going halfway into the rail. Mark this to be removed. This is simpler than it sounds as the diagrams illustrate.

24 Saw down the sides of this block as far as the centre line. Lay the Rail face down on the bench and using a sharp chisel slowly cut away the rest of the block to leave a slot in the Rail. Don't be afraid to turn the rail over and work from the other side as well and don't try to cut away too much at a time.

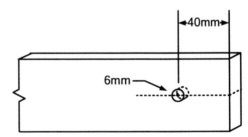

25 Repeat this for 3 of the other Cross Rails.

26 Take **one** of the notched Cross Rails and mark a point 40 mm ($1^5/_8$ in) in from each end and central on the wide face. Using the 6mm bit drill a hole at each of these marks, **both from the same side but only about halfway through** - NOT right through. These will form the housings for the trap door axles. (If you do drill through by accident, you can cut the allthread a little longer so that you can fix nuts on the outside. However you will need to drill right through instep 32 as well)

40mm

6mm

Assembling the Cross Pieces

27 Take a pair of the Cross Rails you've just prepared and place one on the bench with the cut-out upwards. Line up the other Rail so that the cut outs are opposite but at right angles. The width of each cut-out should be the same as the thickness of the Rails.

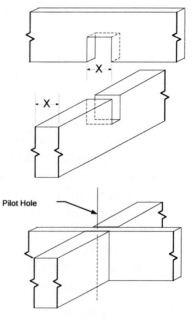

28 Push the two Rails together and the cut-outs will interlock to provide a firm cross shape. Tap home gently with a mallet until the edges are all level. The joint should be tight but don't force the rails together. If the joint seems overly tight, separate the rails and trim the sides of the cut-outs a little, but keep them straight. Do a small amount at a time and test frequently.

Pilot Hole

29 Drill a 3mm pilot hole down through the centre of the cross joint.

30 Repeat for the other pair of Cross Rails so that you have a pair of crosses.

Preparing the Short Rails

31 Take the four short rails and lay them side by side on the bench. Mark the midpoint of the length on all of them and check they line up. Then using a square mark this midpoint line all round on all 4 rails.

Mid-Point Line

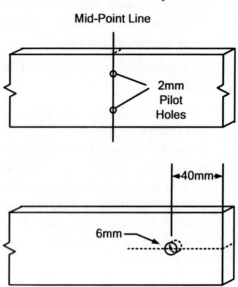

32 Using the 2mm bit, drill pairs of pilot holes along this centre line in the wide face.

2mm Pilot Holes

33 On one of the Short Rails mark a point 40 mm in from each end, central on the wide face. Using the 6mm bit drill a hole at these two marks, both from the same side but only about halfway through - NOT right through. These will form the housings for the trap door axles. (If you do drill through by accident, just cut the allthread a little longer so that you can fix nuts on the outside. However you will need to go back and drill right through in step 26 as well.)

40mm

6mm

Making the Trap Doors

34 Take the 6mm allthread and cut 2 lengths 400mm long. (If you have accidentally made the holes all the way through in step 25 and 30, make these lengths 460mm instead.)

35 Take 2 Trap Door Sides and 2 Trap Door Ends.

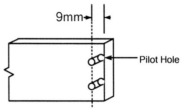

36 Drill two 2mm pilot holes through the each end, of both Door Sides. Drill them through the wide side about 9mm from the ends. Start nails in these holes

37 Stand one of the Door Ends upright on the bench. Take one of the Sides and hold it horizontal with the end positioned on the end of the upright to form a corner. Check that the edges are flush all round and hammer in the nails.

38 Turn the Door Side around so that the other end is near to you and place the other Door Edge vertical under it to make another corner. Again make sure the edges are flush and hammer in the nails.

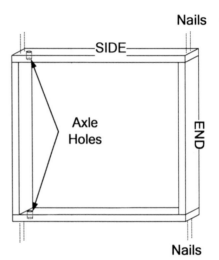

39 Flip the frame over and place the remaining Side piece across the two upright ends. Make sure the edges and ends are flush and hammer in the nails to give you a firm, square frame.

40 Mark a point 25mm (1in) in from one end, along the centre of one of the Sides. Drill a 6mm hole right though. The edge of the hole should be just touching the inside face of the Door End.

41 Turn the frame over and repeat to give a matching, hole on the opposite side.

42 Push one of the lengths of allthread though so that it sticks out evenly on each side.

43 Repeat steps 33 to 41 with the others pairs of Door Sides and Door Ends to make the second door.

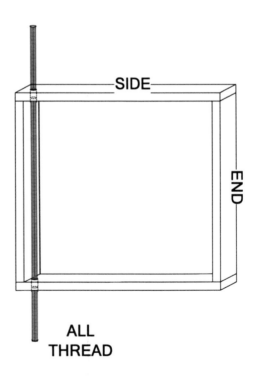

44 Take the 2 smallest pieces of mesh and place one over each trap door. Attached using the stable gun and wire staples. File or trim any sharp edges.

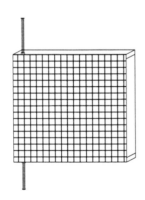

Mounting the Door Springs
If you have not fitted the door mesh at this point it is important that you mark the 'top' of the doors in some way so that you fit them the right way round.

45 The Larsen springs should come in matched pairs as shown. These are torsion springs which generate their power by being would tighter not by being pulled apart.

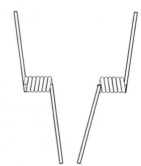

46 Take one Trap Door frame and place it mesh side up on the bench. Select a spring and fit it to the correct side of the Trap Door. It should slide onto the allthread and have both 'arms' on the top with one arm right next to the wooden Side of the Trap Door as shown. If you are unsure, try the springs on both doors until you're happy they are the right way round.

47 Slide the spring right up the wooden frame and hammer in two wire staples to fix the spring arm to the Door Side. The free arm of the spring should be pointing backwards and slightly upwards. If bent round under the allthread the spring should tighten.

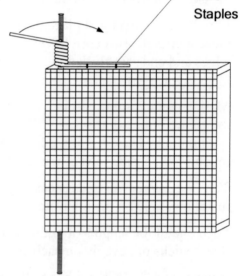

Wire
Staples

48 Repeat for the second trapdoor, you should find that spring fits on the opposite side, giving you a pair of doors like this.   If you have two identical springs then just mount them both on same side of the doors - either both right hand side or both left.

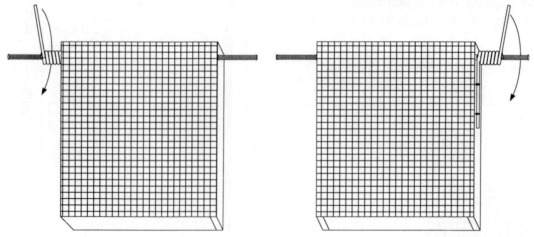

Assembling the frame

By this stage you should have pre-assembled all the parts of the Larsen Trap frame, as shown here. Final assembly requires plenty of room - the finished trap is almost a metre wide and half a metre high. It will also make it easier if you can get someone to help you.

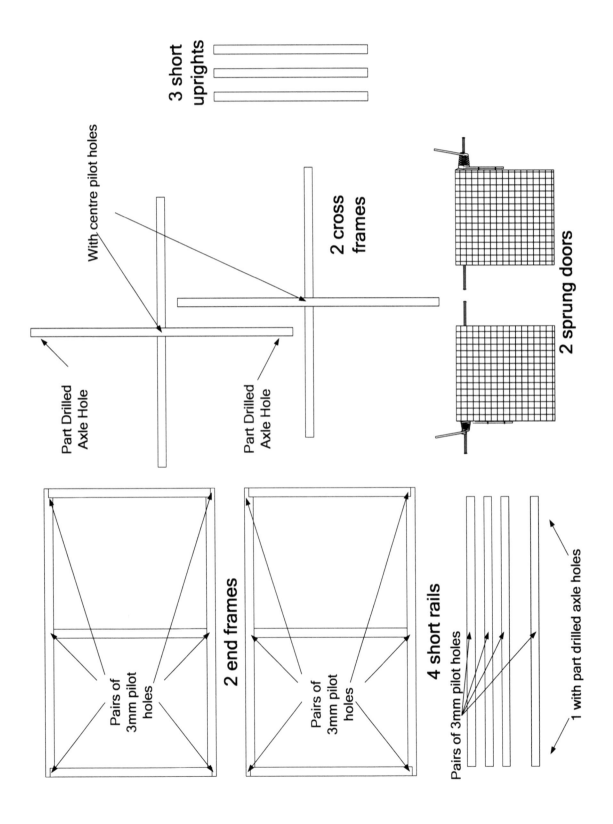

49 Take the Cross Frame which has the part drilled axle holes and lay it on a level surface. Take the Short Rail with the matching holes and lay it opposite - holes in line. Start a couple of nails in the central pilot holes - nailing from the opposite side to the part drilled holes.

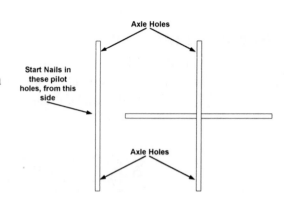

50 Place the two Trap Doors in position; mesh upwards and springs against the outside rail. Push the allthread axles into the Cross Frame axle holes as far as you can.

51 Locate the other end of the allthread axles into the corresponding holes in the Short Rail. Push in hard and if necessary tap in gently with a mallet. The centre of the Short Rail should be firmly against the end of the Cross arm. If not, shorten the allthread slightly.

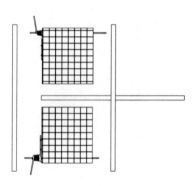

52 Stand the cross up on end so that the free Rail is uppermost. Make sure that it is central and flush with the edges. Hammer in the two started nails.

53 Take another Short Rail and start two nails in the central pilot holes. Turn the cross the other way up so that the doors are now in the bottom half. Position the short rail on the end of the upright cross - check it's flush and central before driving in the nails.

54 Now is when a helper will make things easier. It is also worth taking a few minutes to start off 40mm nails in all the remaining small pilot holes in all the timbers - but not the two large ones.

55 Turn the Cross a quarter turn so that both doors are now on the right hand side, mesh towards you. Your helper should then pick up one of the End Frames. Stood facing you, they should hold the frame so that its top rail sits across the three uprights that you are holding.

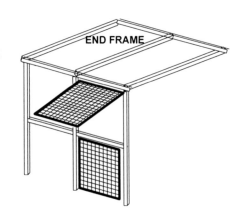

56 Make sure that the connecting pieces are positioned correctly, drive in the nails. Begin with one nail into the central upright, then a single nail at each end, and then finish off the others.

57 While you are doing this you will find that the free arm of the door spring locates against the frame and opens the trap door a bit. This is quite normal. When the trap is complete adjust the spring arm into the frame corners as shown and secure with a wire staple if necessary.

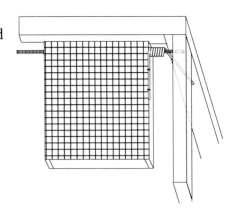

58 Swap places with your helper and place the other crosspiece vertically under the end frame - check positioning and using the pilot holes nail it on. (a) Position a Short Rail either side and carefully nail into the ends of these through the pilot holes. Then roll the trap onto each side in turn to nail these Short Rails onto the end of the cross arms. (b)

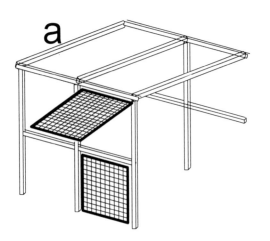

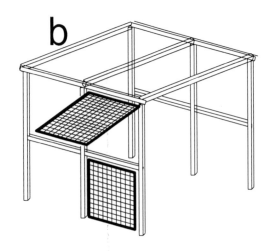

59 Turn the frame right over so that you have 6 'legs' pointing into the air (c). Position the remaining End Frame on top. Check position and nail it down at all six contact points (d)

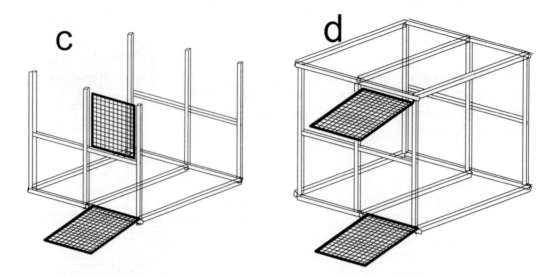

60 All that remains now is to insert the last three uprights. Roll the trap over on its side so that one of the 'open' squares is on the floor. Position a Short Upright against the midpoint line and secure with a corrugated fastener top and bottom. All the short uprights should all be aligned so that the widest part runs along the outside edge.

61 Roll the trap right over and repeat for the other open square.

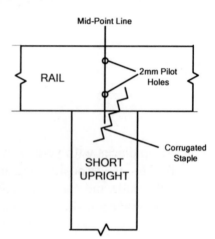

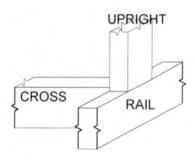

62 Turn the trap back upright and it should look as shown in (e). All uprights in place except the central one.

63 To complete the frame place the final upright between the centres of the Cross Pieces as shown and using a single large nail in each end, fix it in place. Ideally the large width of this central upright should be aligned across the two trap doors, not lined up to run between them. Doing this gives you a flatter frame to attach the mesh to later and means that the plywood divider sits neatly between two uprights.

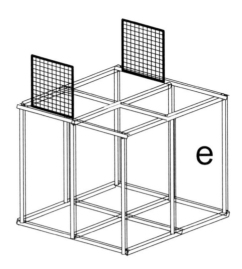

e

CENTRAL UPRIGHT

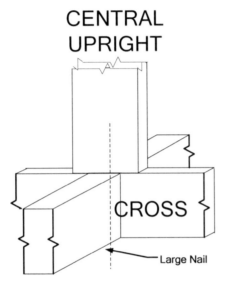

CROSS

Large Nail

You may find that this upright is able to pivot a little on the single nail - this will be tightened up when the mesh and plywood are added

Plywood & Mesh

Adding the plywood.

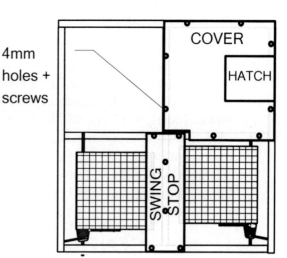

COVER

HATCH

4mm holes + screws

SWING STOP

64 Take the 16 by 5 inch swing stop and drill two 4mm holes along the top and bottom edges; roughly equally spread and 9mm from the edge. Drill two more holes along the long centre line. Push the trap doors inside, position swing stop on the frame trap and secure it with screws. You'll need to hold it down against the springs while you do this.

65 Adjust the position of the free arms of the springs so that they are in the corners and secure with a couple of wire staples.

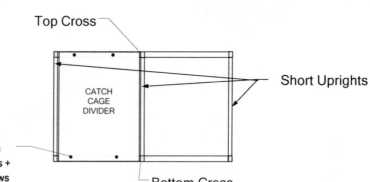

Top Cross

Short Uprights

CATCH CAGE DIVIDER

4mm holes + screws

Bottom Cross

66 Take the 20 by 15 inch plywood divider and drill two 4mm holes along the top and bottom edges; roughly equally spread and 9mm from the edge.

67 Position the divider vertically inside the trap frame, directly beneath the swing stop. It should fit neatly between the Centre Upright and the Short Upright on the outside edge of the frame. Screw the Divider into place.

68 Cut the plywood cover piece as shown. The small notch out of the corner is to fit around the end of the swing stop; it will be about 35mm by 19mm but it's worth just measuring where it fits on your trap before you cut it.

16 inches

6"

5"

6"

5"

69 You have a choice of how you mount the access hatch: The best method is to use the pair of 14 inch pieces of lath and  using a router, cut away matching corners to create a pair of runners. The slots need to be about 3 mm deeper than the thickness of the plywood hatch and about the same distance wide. These rails can be screwed under the cover and the hatch slides back and forth in them. Make sure that you mount them back set in a little from the front and back of the cover to allow them to fit inside the frame.

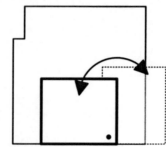

70 A quicker, easier but less sturdy method is to just drill a hole in the corner of the hatch and using a bolt and nut secure it through the cover so that it can be pivoted open and closed.

Adding the mesh

71 Take the long lengths of dowel and cut the ends at 45 degrees. Drill pilot holes through each sloping end and nail in place within the call bird compartment. Shown here from above with call compartment covers removed. Fit them about a third of the way up the compartment.

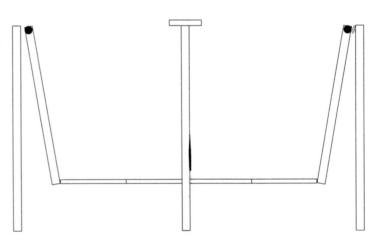
Perches

72 Turn the trap on its side with the Trap Doors in the bottom half. Slide the mesh divider into the frame and position it across the three inside uprights. Combined with the plywood separator already in place, this should divide the trap into the three sections. Carefully staple the mesh all round the edge and along the Central Upright. It will be necessary to trim the mesh at the corners to fit it neatly around the top and bottom rails.

73 Turn the trap back upright and fit the 16 by 16 inch square of mesh over the open square remaining on the trap top. Secure with staples.

74 Turn the trap upside down and fit the 32 by 32 inch square or mesh to the base of the trap. Secure all round the rim and on the cross piece with staples.

75 Finally staple mesh on all four sides. You can do this either by cutting four individual panels or by rolling a continuous sheet of mesh round all four sides. Either way, secure with staples on all edges and uprights and trim off any excess.

Finishing Off

76 With the trap upright, take the two pairs of short dowels, place them end on end against the central dividing board to prop the doors open. Pairs of should be of the same length, i.e. the short ones together and the longer ones together. This is to compensate for the dividing board being mounted on the frame and so slightly to one side.

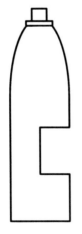

77 The call bird will need water as well as food. Commercial 'cage cups' are produced for aviary birds and these will work very well although being open topped can quickly become contaminated. A very good alternative is to use any 75cl plastic drinks bottle with a segment cut out of the side. This can be secure to the wire mesh with a couple of plastic cable ties.

Options and Variations

Side Opening Doors

An alternative to the top opening design is to have trap doors fitted as side opening. These may be more attractive to crows which like to land a little way away and hop in.
The doors need to be made larger to fit the higher sides about 430mm and the allthread cut longer, about 520mm. The doors are propped open when set, with the split perches positioned between the door and the upright between the doors. The swing stop is fitted <u>inside</u> to prevent the doors going in too far.

Springs Alternatives

If you can't get springs then a strong piece of elasticated rubber or bungee can be a viable alternative. Hooked onto the front of the trap doors and stretched back over the axle, down the side and secured. This type of spring is quickly perishable but easy to replace. However it is weak compared to metal springs and will lose power if left stretched for a long time so should be 'sprung' and tightened frequently.

Using the trap

Obtaining your first call bird can be a challenge. If you know someone else who is operating a Larsen you can sometimes obtain one of their catches, although it is illegal to sell call birds. This is a particularly effective approach as a bird from outside your home territory will be a challenge to any resident birds.

Failing that, magpies can be caught using bait of eggs in a 'fake nest' of straw or dry grass. Scattering broken egg shells or a couple of slices of white bread cut into small cubes, around the trap can also help to attract birds close into the trap.
The importance of caring for the call bird has already been mentioned but is worth emphasising. The bird must be checked daily and given fresh food and water. If the bird is sick or injured it must be humanely dispatched and disposed of appropriately.
As much as possible maintenance of the trap should be done at night. Magpies have sharp eye and particularly in the early days, when you may still have a resident population, you will not want to warn them off. Any caught birds should be removed at night and dispatched away from the trap and out of sight of the call bird.

Chapter 7 – The Pigeon Trap

This trap is of the 'frame and mesh' type described in the introduction. It uses simple passive doors which can be installed in multiples to create a very effective multi-catch trap. The overall cage size can be varied as described later with 'doors' added as required. It is most suitable for control of medium to large scale feral pigeon problems. This design will occasionally capture woodpigeons but not reliably.

The trapping mechanism makes use of a technique that the Pigeon Racing fraternity have been using for years to control the movement of birds in and out of lofts. To make the door a set of light metal rods or 'bob wires' are suspended from the top of the cage opening, approximately a pigeon head width apart. These wires are able to swing freely and independently of each other, but only inwards; a stop bar means that cannot be pushed outwards. Attracted by the bait and other pigeons already in the trap, a bird will push its head between the rods to try and get inside. As it moves forward the wings and shoulders will push the wires forward and upwards with very little effort allowing the bird access. Once past, the rods swing back behind it and are stopped in the vertical position.

On the subject of racing pigeons you may occasionally capture a ringed bird amongst the feral birds. Sometimes this is a racing bird that has joined a feral flock but just as likely it's a bird on route which has stopped for rest and food. Either way any ringed bird should be separated from the others and released as quickly as possible. If a particular bird is recaptured over several days, make a note of the ring number and contact Royal Pigeon Racing Association. Racing pigeons have a high financial and emotional value to their trainers so every effort must be made to return them unharmed.

The Bob Wire Door

Cutting List & Materials

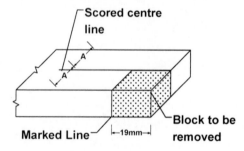

- Lengths of 35mm x18mm roof lath in lengths as below:
    - 1 top rail @ 670mm ($26^3/_8$ inches)
    - 2 outer uprights @ 300mm ($11^6/_8$ inches)
    - 2 base rails @ 120mm (4 ¾ inches)

- Lengths of 70mm x18mm timber in lengths as below:
    - 2 inner uprights @ 300mm ($11^6/_8$ inches)

- 10 x 300mm (12 inch) 'Bob wires'.
    These plans have been created using bobwires which have 40mm wide 'heads' at the top. Check that yours are the same and if not adjust the overall length accordingly leaving a little slack for the rods to move. Similarly if you are using the shorter 230mm (9") bobs adjust the length of the uprights above.)
- 470mm length of 4mm bar or 520 mm length of straight wire at least 2.5 mm thick
- Pack of 40mm galvanised nails.

Tools
- Saw
- Hammer
- Marking gauge
- Chisel & mallet
- Drill with 2mm & 4mm bits
- Screwdriver

Assembly Instructions

Preparation.

1 Take the one of the Outer Uprights and use the marking gauge to make a line along the <u>centre</u> of the wide face at one end. Turn the rail over and at the same end score a matching line on the other side. Be sure to use the gauge from the same edge each time so that the lines are perfectly opposite.

2 Measure in 18mm ($^3/_4$ inch), the width of the lath, from the end of the Upright and using a carpenter's square mark from the centre line out to one edge. Use the square to continue this line onto the edge and across the opposite face until it meets the other scored line.

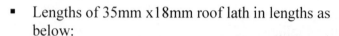

3 Use the square again to join the two scored lines across the very end of the rail and you will have marked a block on the corner of the rail. Shade this with the pencil to indicate which side will be removed.

4   Using two saw cuts, remove this block.

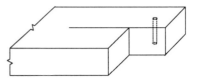

5   Drill one 2mm pilot hole from the top through the shoulder you have just made – drilled through from the wide face.

6   Turn the rail round and repeat at the other end, ensuring that <u>both removed blocks are on the same edge</u>.

7   Repeat steps 1 to 6 for the other Outer Upright <u>and</u> both Base Rails <u>and</u> the Top Rail.

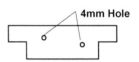

4mm Hole

8   For each **Base Rail**, Drill two 4mm holes through the wide face. These will be used to attach the door to your final cage frame.

9   Next we need to cut housing joints in the Top Rail for the Inner Uprights to fit into. You should already have cut the end joints in Step 7 and the Top Rail should so far look like this.

10 Measure in 102mm (4 in) from the very end and mark a line across the wide face. Mark a second line at 120mm (4 ¾ in) from the same start point. Join this pair of lines together 18mm (¾ in) in from the edge that already has the cut-outs. Use the square to continue the lines onto the edge and across the opposite face and again to a distance of 18mm (¾ in) from the edge. You will end up with a square section marked on one edge and going halfway into the rail. Mark this to be removed.

Line 18mm from edge

18mm

11 Repeat from the opposite end **ensuring** all the cut-outs are on the same side as shown below.

120mm
102mm
18mm
120mm
102mm

12 Saw down the sides of each marked block as far as the line. Lay the Rail face down on the bench and using a sharp chisel slowly cut away the rest of the block to leave a slot in the Rail. Don't be afraid to turn the rail over and work from the other side as well and don't try to cut away too much at a time.

Pilot Hole

13 Finish the Top Rail by drilling a 2mm pilot hole down through the back of each of these slots.

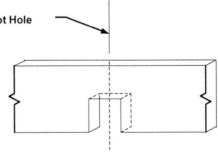

14 Take the two Inner Uprights.
You need to make similar cuts on both ends
of these pieces, again making sure that the
cut-outs are on matching sides.
However as these pieces are wider **do not**
use a centre line. Instead mark a square
block 18mm in from each edge. Mark the
lines all round using a carpenters square.

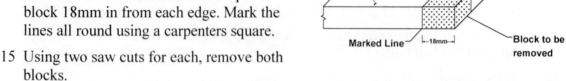

15 Using two saw cuts for each, remove both
blocks.

16 On each Inner Upright mark a point on the wide face; 10mm (3/8 in) in from one end and
25mm (1in) from the uncut edge. Drill a 3mm axle hole at this mark. Place the two
pieces side by side and the holes and cut-outs should all line up.

17 You should be left with pieces looking like this.

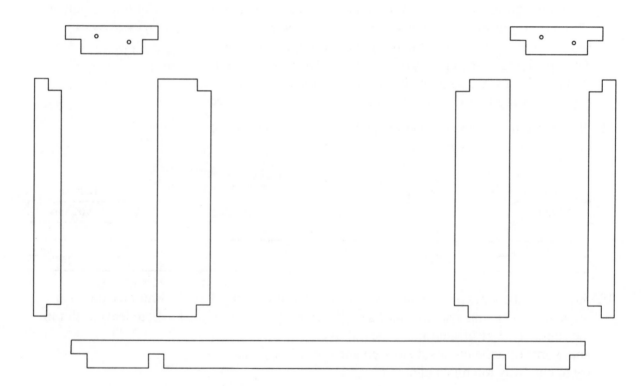

Assembling the Door.

18 Take one Outer Upright and the Top rail; start nails in all the pilot holes.

19 With the Upright vertical on the bench bring the pieces together as shown. Keeping the pieces as tight as you can, drive in the nails – each time rotating the structure so that you are hammering downwards onto a firm surface.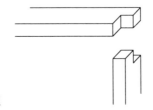

20 Repeat with the other Outer Upright at the other end of the Top Rail.

21 Next place the two Base Rails onto the bottom of the Outer Uprights and nail into place.

22 Finally position the Inner Uprights with the two holes opposite and nearest the Top Rail.

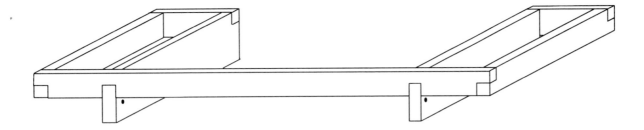

23 Slide one end of the 4mm rod through the hole in one of the Inner Uprights and carefully slide the bobwires onto it. Slide the rod through as you add more until they are all on, then push the rod right through the other hole which should secure it.

24 If using wire instead of rod start by making a right angle bend 25mm from one end as a stop. Once the wire is right through make a similar bend at the other end to lock the wire in place. Be careful not to bend the long length or the bobwires may not swing correctly.

25 Hold the frame upright and check that the bob wires swing freely.
    <u>NOTE</u>: the bobwires will be longer than the frame and so will not swing through if you
    stand the frame on a surface.

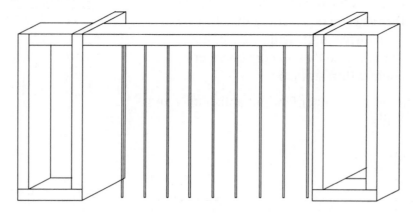

26 The door is now complete but needs to be mounted into the body of the cage. This is
    simply done by placing the door on the bottom edge of your cage and securing it with

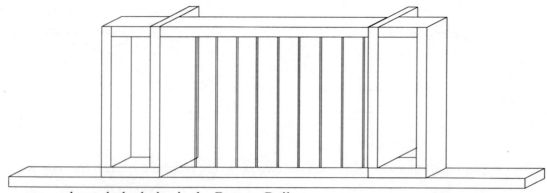

    screws through the holes in the Bottom Rails.

27 Ensure that the back edge of the Door is flush with the back edge of the cage rail so that
    the Bobwires hang down freely and the cage rail acts as a stop to prevent then swinging
    outwards. As this side view illustrates.

28 When the mesh is added to the completed cage is should be cut and fitted round the
    bobwire opening.

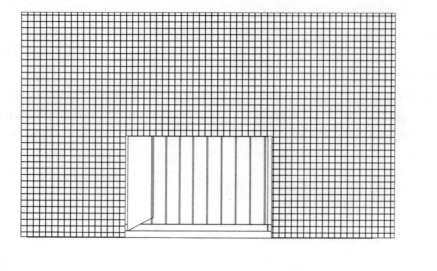

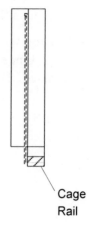

Cage
Rail

Home Made Bob Wires

I prefer to use the commercial ones as they are cheap, reliable and purpose made for the job, but you can make you own which can be just as effective.

The Bent Wire

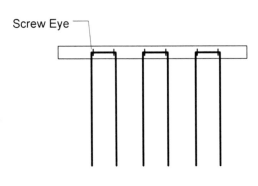

Simply take a piece of 3mm galvanised wire and cut it to a length which is twice the length of the bobwires you want, plus 40mm. Try and get the wire as straight as you can. Then make a right angle bend one 'bob wire' length from each end to give you a long, square 'U' shape with a flat top 40mm across. These can be mounted in a pair of screw eyes fastened to the hanging rail about 35mm apart.

Push one leg of the 'U' through both eyes and slide the whole thing round. Space out the screw eyes so that there is about 45mm between each pair.

The Wound Wire

This method is borrowed from a technique invented by Glenn Waters for making a whole host of things. You need a rig made from a block of hardwood with a hole drilled in it such that you can push a large nail into the hole and it hold firm with about 40 or 50mm sticking out. Drill another hole the same diameter as your wire (about 2 to 3mm); about 15mm deep and 10mm from the nail.

To make the bobwire make a 10mm right angle bend in the end of your wire and push it into the small hole. Keep the wire flat on the surface of the block and bend it round the nail; then keep wrapping the wire round the nail as tight as you can in forming a spiral coil along the length of the nail. Keep going until this coil is 40mm long (between 12 and 20 turns) then slide the whole thing off the nail. Trim the short end close to the spiral and file it smooth. Cut the long end to whatever length you want your bobwire to be. These wire can be slid onto a bar in the same way as the commercial wires but place a washer between each one and the next to avoid the coil ends catching each other

Using The Trap

The trap should be positioned in an area where the pigeons are used to gathering undisturbed – often a flat area of roof space. Bait can be bread, corn, birdseed or anything similar which they're used to feeding on. You should use a fairly large quantity of bait with a pile in the middle of the trap and small amounts scattered around the entrances. Pre-baiting the area for several days before hand will improve the effectiveness.

You should inspect the trap a minimum of daily and more frequently during the first few days. If the weather is hot or if you can only visit early in the day it is good practice to provide some water inside the cage.

Dispatching and removing the birds depends on the size of cage you decide to use. Small cages are built with some sort of access hatch so that birds can be removed and killed individually, either by wringing the neck or by a sharp blow to the back of the head. If you go for a larger cage then it's best to make it big enough to physically get into and deal with them inside. In this situation some basic protective clothing is a good idea as feral pigeons can carry disease and will flap about a lot around you.

Small Cage Pigeon Trap

Commercial pigeon traps using this principle are available made completely from wire mesh; measuring 1m x 600mm by 300mm high (39" by 23" by 12"). You shouldn't make the cages any smaller than that but I prefer even 'small cages' to be a little bigger ; 1m by 600mm square but also 600mm high.

Cutting List & Materials

- Lengths of 35mm x18mm roof lath in lengths as below:
  - 4 Side Rails   @ 1000mm (39 ½ inches)
  - 4 End Rails   @ 786mm (31 inches)
  - 4 uprights   @ 600mm (23 ½ inches)

- Sections of wire mesh
  - Roof section   1000mm by 750mm   (39 ½ inches by 29½ inches)
  - 2 x Sides   1000mm by 600mm   (39 ½ inches by 23 ½ inches)
  - 2 x Sides   750mm by 600mm   (29½ inches by 23 ½ inches)
  - Floor (5mm sq mesh) 1000mm by 750mm   (39 ½ inches by 29½ inches)

- Pack of 40mm galvanised nails.

Tools
- Saw
- Hammer
- Marking gauge
- Drill with 2mm bit
- Staple gun and staples

Assembly Instructions

Preparing the Rails

1 Take the one of the Side Rails and use the marking gauge to make a line along the <u>centre</u> of the wide face at one end. Turn the rail over and at the same end score a matching line on the other side. Be sure to use the gauge from the same edge each time so that the lines are perfectly opposite.

2 Measure in from the end of the rail 35mm (the width of the lath) and using a carpenter's square mark from the centre line out to one edge. Use the square to continue this line onto the edge and across the opposite face until it meets the other scored line.

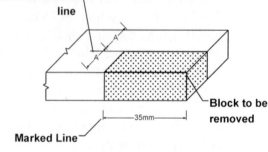

3 Use the square again to join the two scored lines across the very end of the rail and you will have marked a block on the corner of the rail. Shade this with the pencil to indicate which side will be removed.

4 Using two saw cuts, remove this block.

5   Drill two 2mm pilot holes from the top through the shoulder you have just made. Keep them away from the rail end as other holes will be needed here.

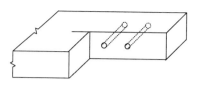

6   Turn the rail round and repeat at the other end, ensuring that <u>both removed blocks are on the same edge</u>.

7   Repeat steps 1 to 6 for all four Long Rails.

Assembling the frame Top and Base.

8   Bring together two of the Side Rails and two of the Ends.

9   Start a nails in one of the pilot holes at each end of the End Rails.

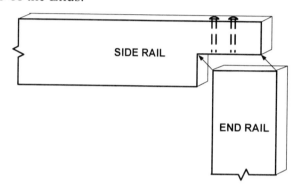

10 Place the End Rail vertical on the floor. Taking a Side Rail fit the housing you made onto the end of the End Rail. It should fit neatly into the cut-out, with the end of the End Rail in contact with the pilot holes. Keeping the pieces as tight as you can, drive in the nail.

11 Turn the rail around and fit the other End Rail into the other end and drive in the nail.

12 Flip the structure over so that the first Side Rail is now on the bench and the End Rails are sticking up in the air. Locate the second Side Rail onto the uprights pieces in the same way and drive in the nails.

13 Go back round all four corners and drive nails into the four remaining pilot holes at these joints.

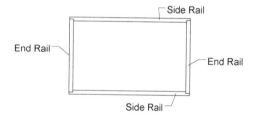

14 You should now have a firm rectangular frame which will form the base of your cage.

15 Using the 2mm bit, drill pairs of pilot holes at each corner about 9mm in from the end of the top and bottom rails.

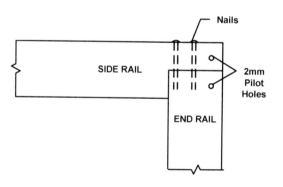

16 Repeat steps 9 to 19 to make a matching frame for the top of your cage end frame.

Final Assembly.

17 Place one frame flat on the floor or bench and start nails in all the pilot holes in all four corners.

18 Gather together the 4 uprights and then get someone to help you with the next part.

19 Hold one of the uprights vertical on a firm surface and position a corner of the prepared frame over the end of the upright.   Align the Upright so that the larger width extends over both the pilot holes and crosses the joint in the frame corner. Drive in the nails.

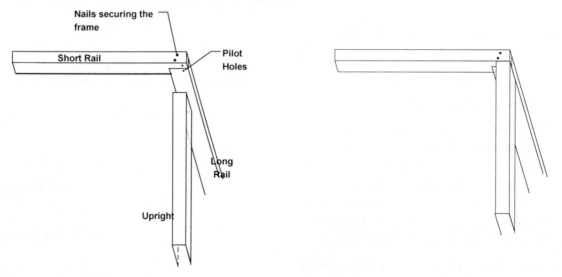

20 Repeat for all four corners and turn the frame over so that the Uprights are sticking up in the air.

21 Start nails in the pilot holes in each corner of the Top Frame. Take the frame and locate it onto the uprights pieces in the same way and drive in the nails. This gives you your final completed cage frame.

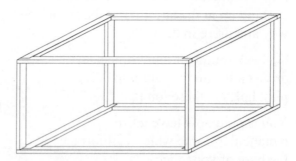

22 Fix the Bobwire doors in place on one or both of the long sides. <u>If you fit it to the short side you probably won't be able to reach all the way inside.</u>

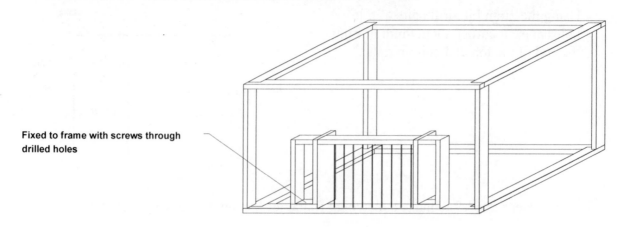

Fixed to frame with screws through
drilled holes

23 Fix the mesh in place, around the opening of the doors.

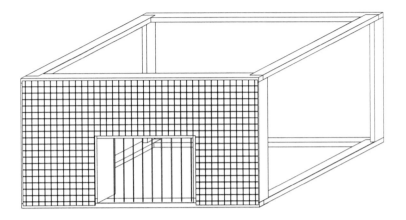

24 And then on the top and remaining sides.

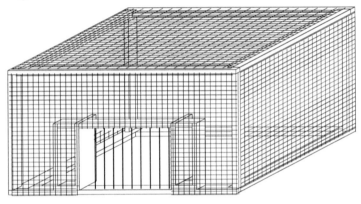

25 Turn the trap over and add the fine mesh panel across the base of the cage. The finer mesh for the base is to make it more comfortable for the trapped birds and allow their behaviour to be more relaxed and natural

Operating the trap

The trap is self setting – just put it out baited and check regularly as described. To empty the cage, simply tip it backwards so that the bobwire door is top most. If you've put two doors on opposite sides don't worry; the downward bobs will just stay closed.   Reach in and carefully and remove one bird at a time. I have found it helpful to have a piece of plywood to hand to pop over the hole as a temporary cover while you deal with each removed bird.

Large Cage Pigeon Trap

Making a larger Pigeon cage can be as simple as increasing the overall lengths of the rails and uprights given for the small cage. As long as the timber is the same thickness and width, all the joint measurements will be the same.   However if the shortest side is much longer that 600mm you will find it difficult to reach the corners of the trap from the entrance hole.
To get round this you will need to add a central access hatch – balancing easy of access against the risk of having birds escape past you.

Alternatively make a large cage as described in the next chapter fitted with bobwires and a plain top.

Remember to fit the bobwire doors before you add the mesh

Chapter 8 - Large Cage Bird Traps

If you really need a large pigeon trap, like the one in the photograph, it is worth making a cage with a door and that is big enough to physically get inside. The simplest way to create this large cage is to build five separate panels that are bolted together on site – four sides and a roof.

An advantage of this approach is that you can make a set of different trap tops which are interchangeable on the same cage frame. This gives you a flexible trap that you can easily change to make into a range of different types. This chapter shows you how to make a basic 'Large Frame' which with bobwires fitted and a plain top can be used as a large pigeon trap. There are then instructions for making cage tops which will create a 'Funnel Trap' and a 'Ladder Trap'. These different tops assume the cage dimensions given for the Basic Large Cage, but you can easily adapt them to suit any size cage you like.

Roof lath is still adequate as a material for these very large traps although you will require some bracing and sometimes additional uprights in the frames. Larger timber can also be used but avoid going thicker than 40mm on the narrowest width if you can as this will create a large 'step up' to a bobwire door.

As with all traps you should inspect it a minimum of daily and more frequently during the first few days. If the weather is hot or if you can only visit early in the day it is good practice to provide some water inside the cage.

Basic Large Cage

Cutting list & Materials

Cut for lengths of timber for each side panel; two uprights and two top / bottom rails.
Remember to make these into matching pairs of opposite sides
e.g. For a cage 2m by 3m and 2m high you will need:

Side 1: 2 x 2m rails, 2 x 2m uprights
Side 2: 2 x 3m rails, 2 x 2m uprights
Side 3: As side 1
Side 4: As side 2
Top: 2 x 2070 mm rails, 2 x 3070mm rails
(The extra length is because the top will need to extend over the corner posts.)

- 16 x m6 bolts long enough to go through the frame width and post. (80mm)
- 8 x m6 bolts long enough to go through twice the frame width. (60mm)
- 24 x m6 wing nuts
- 40mm galvanised nails
- Wire mesh to cover
- Plywood and screws for corner braces

Making the Side Panels

The side panels are made using the halving joints you should now be familiar with and use the wider face as the outer edge.

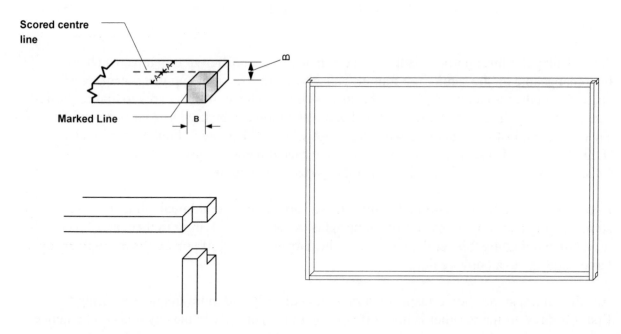

My preferred way to brace these large panels is by using plywood 'corners' screwed on to the frame to support the joints. Make these corners with 200mm to 300mm long sides or larger.

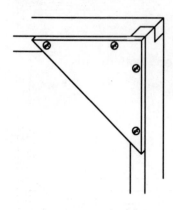

An alternative is an additional piece of lath cut to fit diagonally corner to corner.

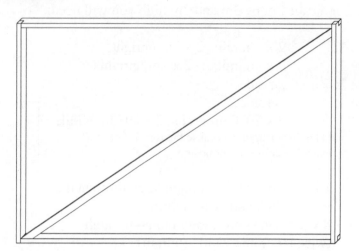

Fitting a Door

Make the door in exactly the same way that you've made the sides – halving joints in the corners and make the door a little shorter than the inside height of the side you're fitting to – remember it has to fit inside the frame.

You will also need to create a 'door pillar' to close the door against but this is simply another 'upright' jointed mid rail.

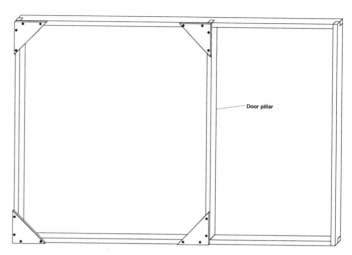

Door pillar

The door needs to fit with enough space to be able to open without catching on the door pillar.

Hinge it to the outside of the frame and secure with a bolt or hasp and staple. It is sometime helpful to be able to padlock the door if there is regular access to the area by other people.

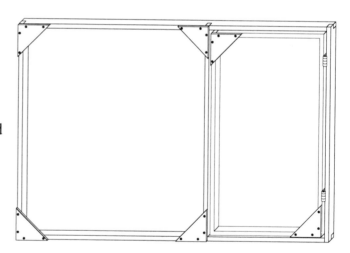

Making a Plain Top.

The trap top is just another frame but you want the rails to be 'wide face down' so that it fits neatly onto the sides. You can see detailed instructions for making this type of frame in steps 1 to 16 of the Larsen Trap plans.

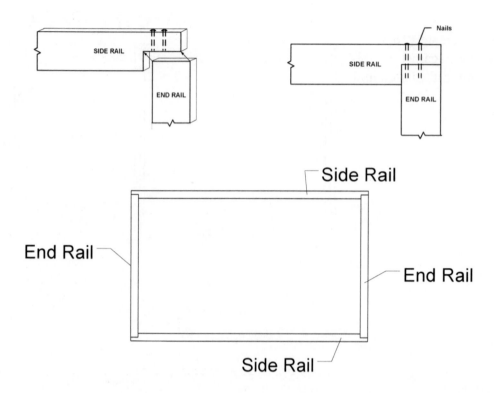

The lengths for the Top sides and ends are slightly longer than those of the frame as these have to include the extra length created by the corner posts.

Assembling into a cage

1 To connect these panels into the cage you'll need four corner posts. These should be the full height of the cage and of square section; the same width as the frame side. So if you've made the frames from roof lath the posts will be 35mm by 35mm.

2 Drill 2 or 3 holes through the side uprights of each frame - evenly spaced and don't make them the same height on both uprights. For example on a 2m high frame drill the left hand holes at 500mm, 1000mm and 1500mm and on the right hand side use something like 200mm, 900mm and 1700mm. The measurements don't need to be exactly this but you just need to make sure the holes don't clash.

3 Begin by positioning one of the corner posts against the left hand side of one of the frames. Line it up and mark through the holes onto the posts. Drill holes right through the post at these marks and fix the frame to the post using bolts and wing nuts.

4 Now position the right hand side of another frame against the post – but not the opposite face. The wing nuts would be in the way anyway.

5 Again mark and drill the holes. You can see now that if the holes were all the same height the bolts would be in the way of each other. Bolt this frame to the post as well and you now have a corner.

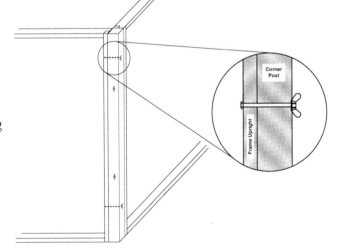

6 Take another post and using the same method attach it to the end of one of the frames. Ensure that it is flush all round.

7 Next attach a third frame to this post in the same way. This frame should be parallel with the first frame giving you three sides of the rectangular cage.

8 Then attach the two remaining posts to the 'spare' ends of the first and third frame.

9 Finally fit the last frame between the two posts.

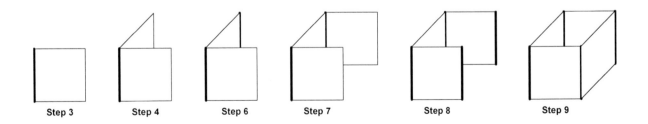

10 Place the cage top on top of the frame and it should be flush all the way round.

11 Fix it in place using the same 'bolt through' method only this time you are bolting through the edges of the Top into the top rail of each 'side'. You will need slightly short bolts for this.

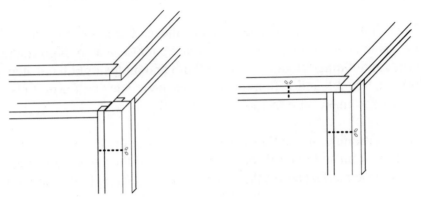

12 It is a really good idea at this point to label how the pieces fit together by putting pairs of corresponding numbers at each join. This also helps to ensure that the frames are the right way up when you next assemble it – particularly useful if you have just transported it in a van or on a roof rack.

Adding the Mesh

It is much easier to fit the mesh after this frame has been assembled for the first time so that you have maximum access when you're drilling the holes. You can either dismantle the frame again into sections to add mesh or apply it as is. However remember to cut and **fix the mesh only to the frames, not the corner posts**. If you go over the joins between sections you won't be able to dismantle the trap again.

Once you're familiar with this construction technique you will probably be able to make each panel completely before assembly.

Options and Variations

You can add extra uprights or cross pieces to any of the frames if extra support is required. These can be jointed like the Inner Uprights of the Bobwire Door (p67).

Alternatively they can be simply held in place by corrugated fasteners, as in the Larsen Trap sides (p52) or by nails through pilot holes in the main rails, as in the Larsen trap door (p54).

Funnel Trap

The funnel trap is a Passive Door which relies on birds landing in the trap top and then dropping down through the funnel to feed. Once inside they have to be airborne to reach the funnel again to get out but with wings open they cannot fit back through.

This design assumes a cage of the size given for a Basic Large Cage earlier in this chapter. If you want to fit it to a different size cage it is fine to alter supports but any changes to the funnel need to be done carefully.

The original specifications laid down by MAFF during the 1960s for a 'Rook, Crow and Jackdaw' trap has a funnel which tapers to 200mm square. In practice Crows can escape through smaller holes than Rooks, and Jackdaws through even smaller ones, so in these plans I have reduced the opening to 150mm square. Depending on your target species you may want to adjust the width of the bottom edge of the mesh panels down to 75mm for Jackdaws. You can also adapt the larger funnel by making an inner cone which tapers to the smaller hole and just dropping it inside the fixed one.

Cutting list & Tools

Cut lengths of roof lath and the 4 mesh panels to the dimensions given below.

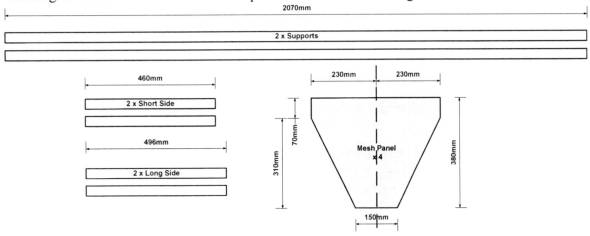

- Sections of wire mesh
    - Roof section   3070mm by 2070mm
- 8 x 40mm galvanised nails.
- 8 x 40mm size 6 screws

Tools
- Saw
- Hammer
- Marking gauge
- Drill with 2mm bit
- Staple gun and staples

Assembly Instructions

Making the Funnel

1 Take the two Long Sides and drill two pilot holes through the wide face – roughly a third of the way in from each end and along the centre.

2 Then drill two 2mm pilot holes through the each end. Drill them through the wide side about 9mm from the ends. Start nails in these holes

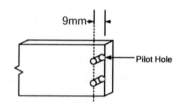

3 Take one of the Short Side and lay it narrow side down on the bench. Place one of the pieces of mesh on top of the rail making sure that the long top edge of the mesh is flush with the back edge and sides. Secure the mesh with staples.

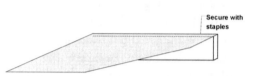

4 Roll the Short Side backwards onto its wide face with the mesh sticking upwards. Bend the mesh downward across the wide face of the rail and secure with staples.

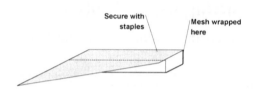

5 Repeat for the second Short side.

6 Repeat for Both Long Sides but position the wire in the middle of the length – there should be an 18mm gap at either end.

7 Stand one of the Short Side upright on the bench, mesh on the left. Take one of the Long Sides and hold it horizontal, mesh downwards, with the end positioned on the end of the short side to form a corner. Check that the edges are flush all round and hammer in the nails.

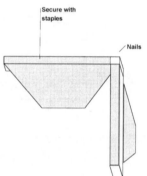

8 Turn the Long Side around so that the other end is near to you and place the other Short Side vertical under it to make another corner – mesh inside the square you're making. Again make sure the edges are flush and hammer in the nails.

9 Flip the frame over and place the remaining Side piece across the two upright ends. Make sure the edges and ends are flush and hammer in the nails to give you a firm, square frame.

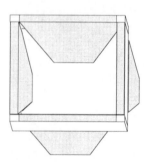

10 You will be left with a square frame with mesh attached to the top and bent round onto the inner faces.

11 Turn the whole frame over so that the mesh
    pieces stick upwards into the air. Draw
    together the top edges of the four mesh pieces
    to form a square.

12 Secure the joins between the mesh sheets
    using cable ties.

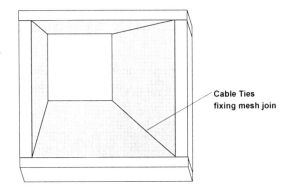

Cable Ties
fixing mesh join

Mounting the Funnel

13 Take one of the Support rails and measure the mid point. Then mark lines 240mm either
    side of that center on one wide face.
    Repeat for the second Support.

14 Lay the Support wide side down on the bench and position the Funnel between the two
    marks, with one pair of screw holes against the Support.

15 Checking that the top if the Funnel is flush with the edge of the rail, screw into position.

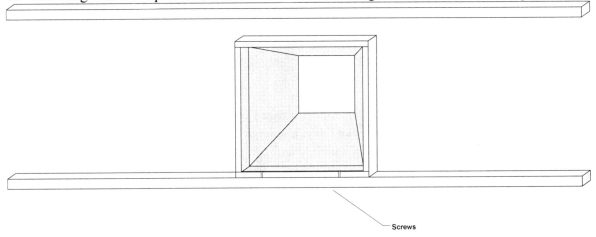

Screws

16 Repeat to add the second rail

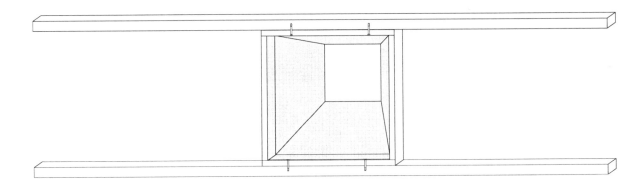

17 Position the funnel and supports across a plain top which is already fitted with mesh.   Cut a whole in the mesh to fit the tunnel and screw the supports onto the top of the frame.

18 Turn the trap over and staple the mesh around the funnel frame from the underside. Shown here with a section of mesh cut away for visibility

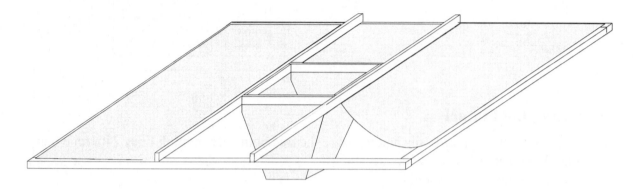

Options and Variations

One option is fit the supports into the frame from the beginning using halving joints or similar.   The advantage of having the supports raised above the mesh is that they provide interested birds with convenient perches where they can investigate the trap before entering the tunnel.   Without these it may be difficult to get birds to enter the funnel.

This type of trap works best if there are also entrances at ground level. If you have fitted Bobwire doors to your Large Cage leave them active as they may work once the first few birds have been caught.   Alternatively make tunnels as described on page 35 but with a wide shoulder round the entrance and push these through the Bobwire doors.

Operating the trap

Place the cage in an area where the birds are already feeding – leave the lid off and bait the open cage for several consecutive days.   Once the birds are feeding regularly fit the trap top at dusk and rebait.

The bait should be whatever the birds are feeding on – wheat, bread or carrion are often effective.

Ladder Trap

The Ladder Trap is a very effective example of the passive door at work. Birds will land on and around the trap attracted by the bait and previous catches. Eventually they will find the 'ladder'; not a ladder in the usual sense but a ladder shaped section in the trap top with holes just big enough to get through. Just like the funnel trap, birds with folded wings can drop through but cannot fly back out.

The spacing of the 'rungs' is the key as you need to get the holes just the right size; for crows you want a gap of 150mm between the rungs, for jackdaws it's just 75mm. You can make two ladders and swap the over as you need to.

This plan is for the 150mm gap but can easily be adjusted by decreasing the distance in steps 5 and 6.

At either end of the ladder the rungs are closer together; it will still look like way out but the holes will be too small to climb through. If this section were blocked completely birds would be encouraged to try the first visible 'gap' which actually would be big enough to pass through.

The second key feature of this trap is that the sides and top of the trap extend upwards past the height of the ladder. Any birds flying to the highest point in the cage are going past any available opening. Wire mesh 'skirts' hung down either side of the ladder also deflect birds away.

In this section I have explained how to make a Ladder Top which will fit with the Large Cage that runs through this chapter. If you want to build a dedicated ladder trap read through to the Options before you start building as the design can be simplified.

Making the Ladder

The ladder is very simple to make provided that you apply a little thought before you start.

You will need 2 pieces of lath long enough to run the full length of the cage, including the width of the end frames. So for a cage of the dimensions used so far each one would be 3070mm.

You then need a set of ladder 'rungs', again lath but of length 130mm. For the 3 metre run you'll need about 25 to 50 of these depending on the ladder you want

Finally you need four 500mm corner posts matching the ones you used for the Large Cage.

Rather than give a set of measurements for the 3m ladder I am going to explain how to work out the spacing yourself so that you can work with any length of ladder.

Begin by marking the 'False Exits' at either end of the ladder

1   Take one of the long Ladder Side lengths and place it on the bench narrow side upwards. Measure along from one end a distance equal to the width of the frame plus 40mm. (Using the Large Cage discussed so far that would be 35mm + 40mm = 75mm). Make a mark at this point.

2   Now measure along from that point a distance equal to the width of a ladder 'rung' plus a 40mm space. As we're using the rungs narrow side up, for the Large Cage this will be 40mm +18mm = 58mm. Mark a line at this point.

3   Measure and mark a further two 58mm spaces.

4   Repeat steps 1 to 3 at the other end of the Ladder Side.

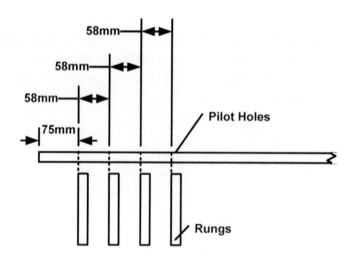

Marking the remaining rungs positions.

5　Now find the centre of the Ladder Side and mark lines either side of it at distance 75mm plus the width of a rung (75mm + 18mm = 93mm).

6　Then mark another point at a distance from that equal to the width of a ladder 'rung' plus a 150mm space. (150mm + 18mm = 168mm). Continue to mark further points separated by this distance until you get near to the lines marked in step 3.

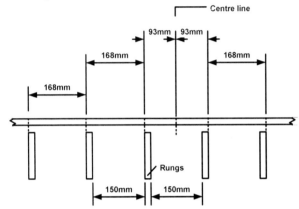

7　As you bring the two sets of lines together you'll end up with a final gap, marked as 'X' on the diagram. If you're lucky this will be an exact match for one of your spacings (168mm or 58mm in our case), but chances are it will be some thing different. If it's somewhere between the two sizes then that's fine. If the gap is too small then move the last mark to the midpoint of the remaining space. Ensuring that the gaps are all less than 150mm once the rungs are fitted. This example illustrates; space 'X' is too small so the rung is centred in the available gap.

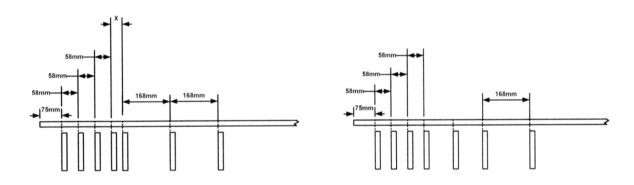

8　Repeat for the other Ladder Side.

9　Having completed this drill pairs of vertical pilot holes just inwards of each mark.

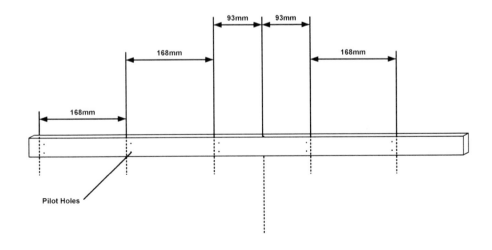

Fixing the Rungs

10 Now attach the rungs by nailing through the pilot holes into the end of the rungs. Aligning the edges of the rungs to the marked lines. Remember that the rungs go inside the marks so start in the middle and work out towards one end. Then return to the middle and work to the other. This prevents you getting confused as to which side to position each one.

11 Position the second ladder side and nail in to a rung at each end. Then work your way along checking the position of each rung as you go.

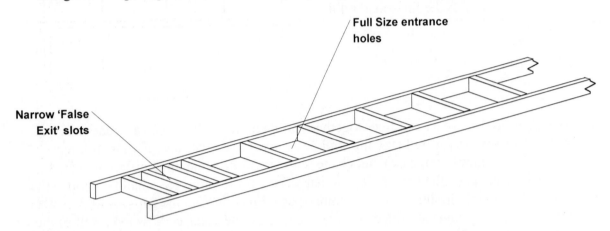

Making the skirts

The effectiveness of the Ladder can be enhanced by adding wire mesh 'skirts' on either side. These are a type of 'baffle' and help to prevent birds getting back through the entry holes. The skirts should be made of light weight but tight mesh, (holes about 10mm square or smaller), and should run the full length of the ladder and extend down 300mm.

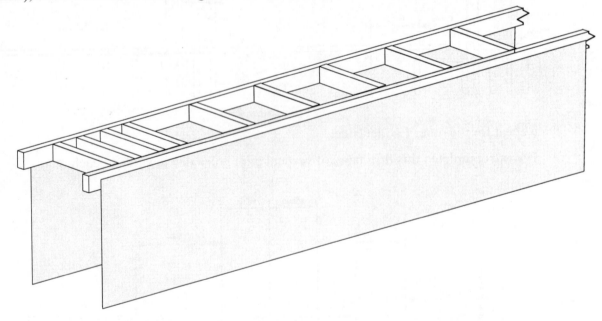

Making the Rest of the Frame

To convert our Large Cage into a Ladder Trap we need to build extensions to the sides as well as a pair of panels to close in the top. These extension sides are joined together just like the sides of the Large Cage; either screwed or bolted to corner posts.

For the long sides all that is required are two smaller rectangular frames of the same constructions as the main cage sides. Make these the same length but only 500mm high.

These will sit directly on top of the main cage sides and be bolted onto the top rail of the cage and a short corner post.

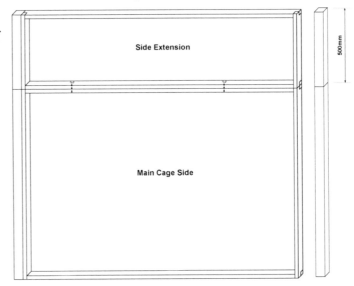

For the ends of the trap top we need to create the framework the sloping mesh which rises up from the ladder to the higher cage sides. It needs to look like this

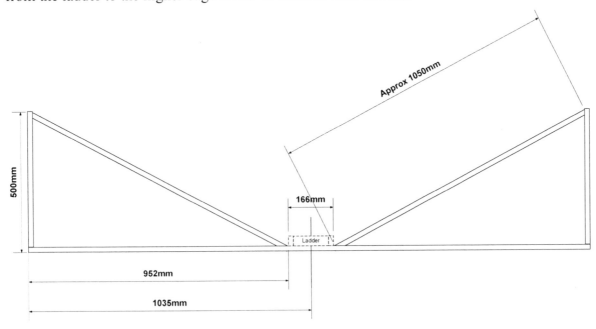

Take a length of lath that will run the full width (2070mm), place this Rail wide face upwards and make the centre.

Position the end of your ladder on this centre line and mark the edges of the ladder on the Rail. Put the ladder to one side.

At each end of the Rail use a halving joint to fit a 500mm length of lath as an Upright. Up to now this is just like making all the other frames. The tricky bit is adding the diagonal pieces.

Making sure that the Uprights and Rail are at right angles measure the distance from the top of the Upright to the nearest ladder edge mark.

Take a piece of lath a little over that length and place it narrow edge down on the bench. Lay the Rail / Upright frame on top of it.

Position it all so that the top edge of the diagonal lath is lined up with the top of the Upright and the ladder mark. Using a pencil draw along the inside edge of the frame to mark the angle at which you need to trim the diagonal.

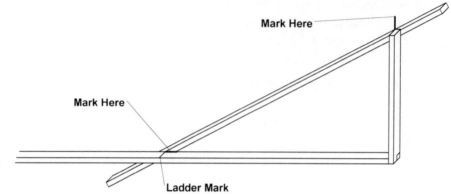

Use a carpenters square to follow both lines right round the lath and then cut it to the marked angle.

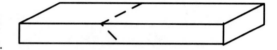

The cut piece should now fit inside the frame and can be screwed into place.

Do the same for the other side and check that the frame is square at the corners and that the ladder fits in the gap between the diagonals.

Repeat to create the second end frame.

Assemble the top by screwing or bolting each frame in turn to the four short corner posts.

Position and fix the ladder.

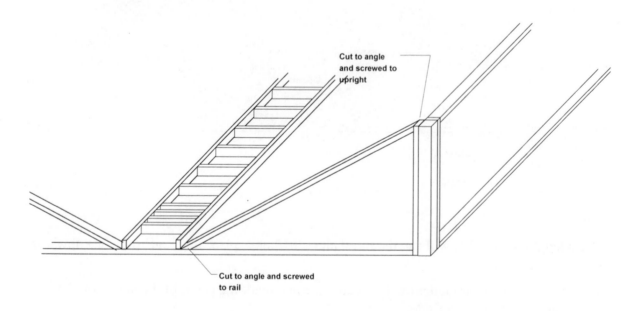

Complete the trap by covering all the sides and the sloping roof sections with wire mesh. Do not cover the ladder

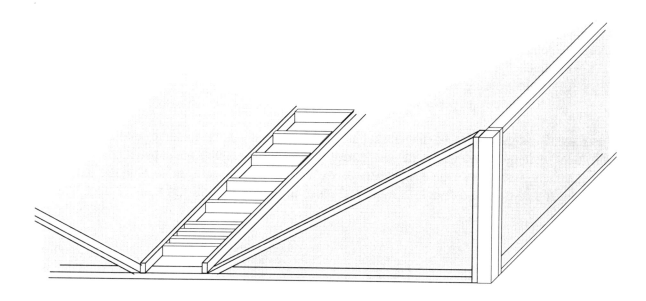

For the final assembly position the whole top onto the Large Cage Frame and screw or bolt to the top rails of the cage sides.

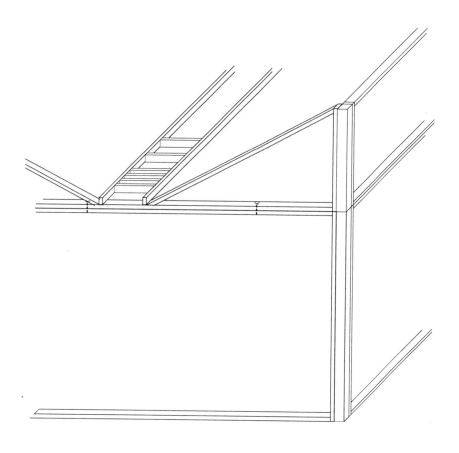

Options and Variations

The plans above take you through making a full top that you can fit on top of the Large Cage featured right through this chapter.

If you wanted to make a dedicated Ladder Trap it can be simpler.
- Make each of the four sides as a complete frame incorporating the basic cage side and the corresponding bit of the trap top.
- Use longer corner posts which go the full height.

If you still want the trap to be dismantled into sections then you will need to make two additional rectangular frames to lie on the roof and hold the sloping mesh panels. If you simply attach mesh across the end frames, as we've done here, you'll be joining the panels together. It's also quite difficult to staple the mesh on to the top of a full height trap.

Operating the trap

Place the cage in an area where the birds are already feeding – leave the lid off and bait the open cage for several consecutive days. Once the birds are feeding regularly fit the trap top at dusk and rebait.

The bait should be whatever the birds are feeding on – wheat, bread or carrion are often effective.

Chapter 9 – Spring Trap Tunnels

This chapter provides plans and information for items which are not strictly traps in their own right, but which are still trapping equipment.

A 'fenn' trap tunnel

The 1995 Spring Trap Approval Order details which spring traps may be used for which quarry and sets out any specific rules on how they must be used. The order states that spring traps of this particular type *"must be set in a natural or artificial tunnel which is suitable for minimising the chances of injuring or killing non-target species whilst not compromising the capture and killing of target species."*

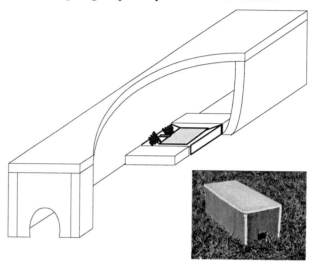

This plan is for a tunnel suitable for the Fenn, Springer and Solway types but can easily be adapted to suit the other approved traps and even regular rat and mouse 'break back' traps.

The traps are available in to different sizes, which relate back to the original Fenn model numbers the Mark 4 and the Mark 6. Size 4 are approved for use on grey squirrels, stoats, weasels, rats, mice while the slightly larger and more powerful size 6 is approved for mink in addition to those listed for the Mark 4.

By using a tunnel you are trying to achieve 3 things:
- Make it wide enough to fit the trap and unhooked safety catch but without allowing space to pass by the side.
- Make it high enough for the trap to fit when fired, but not allowing the quarry to escape over the top or be foul caught.
- Minimise the opportunity for non-target species to be caught through suitable length and 'fencing'.

Plywood is a very suitable material for portable tunnels but doesn't need to be thicker than 9mm – thinner than other traps in this book. Use waterproof marine grade and treat it with a non-creosote preservative.

The tunnel is made 3 sided, leaving the floor natural as some animals find this more acceptable. It also means that if the soil is soft enough the trap can be 'bedded in'. Two short lengths of roofing lath are used in the middle of the tunnel floor to add rigidity to the structure but also are spaced in such a way as to fit the set trap between them, this has a beneficial effect by making the animals almost climb onto the trap plate.

'Fencing' is the term for restricting the tunnel opening to allow in only rats, squirrels or other quarry species - these plans use a plywood panel with a hole cut in.

Tunnels can be made of many materials and more permanent natural tunnels from rocks, bricks, logs or other natural features can be very effective.

Cutting List & Materials

- Outer box pieces in **9mm** exterior grade plywood cut as shown.
  (If you use 12mm just make the top 6mm wider)
- 2 x pieces of roof lath Jump Sticks length 'D'
- 30mm oval nails

Tools

- Saw
- Hammer
- Screwdriver

Optional Tools

Jigsaw or coping saw

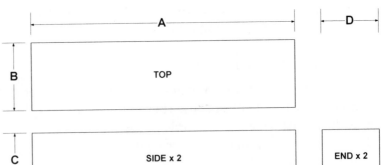

Minimum length in MM (Inches)	A Length	B Width	C Height	D Inner width
'Mark 4' size	760mm (30 in)	183mm (7 ¼ in)	155mm (6 in)	165mm (6 ½ in)
'Mark 6' size	760mm (30 in)	208mm (8 ¼ in)	180mm (7 in)	190mm (7 ½ in)

Assembly Instructions

1. Take the tunnel Top board and mark a line about 5mm (3/16 in) in from each of the long edges. Drill 3mm pilot holes at roughly equal intervals and then take ten nails, (five along each side), and start the nails off in the pilot holes

2. Add two pilot holes at each end, the same distance in from the board edge.

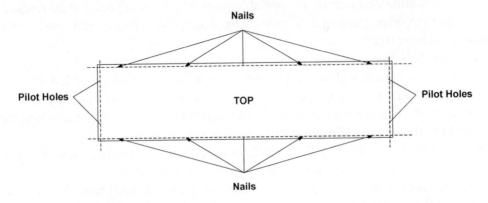

3. Take each Side piece and mark the centre. Mark a line 75mm (3") (70mm for MK4) each side of the centre and another line 35mm (1 ³/₈") outside that. These are the guide lines for the jump rails. Drill two 3mm pilot holes between each pair of line and 9mm (³/₈") up from the bottom edge.

4. Drill pairs of pilot holes at end of the two side pieces, similar to those done for the roof.

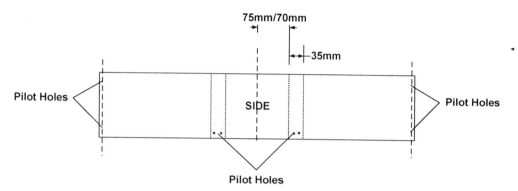

5. Stand the two sides 'on edge' on the bench and about the right distance apart, hole at the bottom and opposite as picture above.
    Place the Top in position, nails up. Carefully line up each Side with the Top and hammer in the 5 nails for that Side. Then repeat for the other side and you should have the basic box shape.

6. Take each of the End Pieces and mark the centre of edge 'D' and then measure 25mm (1") either side of the centre point. At each of these points use a carpenters square to draw a 50mm (2") line at right angles to the 'D' edge. Join these lines across the top to form a square. **For Rabbit & Mink don't bother with the end pieces.**

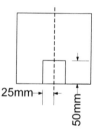

7. Using two saw cuts and a jigsaw or coping saw cut this square out of both Ends. If you prefer you can curve the top a little to make an arch shape.

8. Stand the Tunnel upright and position one End piece in the end of the Tunnel, cut-out downwards. Check that it is flush with the end of the tunnel and hammer in nails from the Top. Turn the Tunnel on each side in turn and hammer in the nails.

9. Repeat for the other End Piece.

10. Place one of the Jump Sticks inside the Tunnel; wide side downwards and flush against the bottom of the tunnel. The end of the Jump stick should be between one pair of guide lines. Hammer nails through the two pilot holes on each side

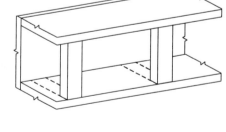

11. Repeat for the other jump stick to complete the tunnel.

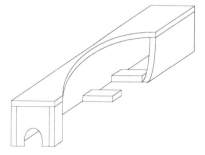

Options and Variations

Improving Access

The basic tunnel described in the plan is very easy to make but has shortcomings in some situations as it is necessary to lift the whole tunnel every time the trap has fired or periodically release and reset it. It can also be difficult to check the trap in situ and to release the safety catch. There are two simple options than can reduce this problem:

Fully Removable lid

By making the whole top 25mm (1") wider it will hang over either side of the tunnel by about the plywood width on either side. A short length of 25mm wide ply can then be attached each side to hold the top in place. To inspect the trap the whole lid can be lifted off or slid along out of the way.

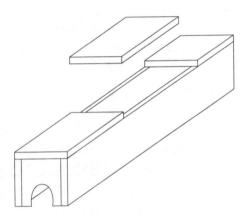

Partly Removable lid

Another option is to cut the original lid into three sections – the middle section corresponding to the outside edges of the jump sticks. The two end sections are nailed on as before, but the middle 'access door' is held in place by turn buttons or similar catches and can be removed whenever necessary. This is ideal for a permanent tunnel set as the tunnel entrances can be covered with soil or other material to create a more natural tunnel.

Length

If the tunnel is to be used as a baited 'blind' tunnel (i.e. closed at one end) the overall length can be reduced down to about 460mm (18"). One plywood end is left uncut without an opening.

Fencing Options

The plywood ends can be replaced with weld mesh stapled to the end of the tunnel. This can either be 50mm (2") squares which would be the right size of the quarry or smaller mesh with a suitable hole cut into it.

If you do use mesh it and a fully removable top you will need to use two extra pieces of lath, same size as the jump sticks, positioned at the top to support the tunnel shape.

Signals

Consider including a 'signal' to indicate when the trap has fired.

Setting Stick

Make a hazel setting stick, about 460mm (18") long, to knock off the trap safety catch once the tunnel is in place.

Other Spring Trap Boxes

Even normal rat traps are safer and often more effective if housed in some sort of box.   This enables you to put the traps outside without worrying about birds, pets or children's fingers. The following diagrams give some ideas of layouts; again 9mm or 12mm plywood is quite sufficient for these and nailed together like the tunnel.   All the boxes should be provided with lids slightly larger than the box itself to give an overhang to protect from the weather.

Make the trap housings to fit your traps, allowing about an extra 10mm clearance at the side. You could also consider fitting a small jump stick in front of the traps.

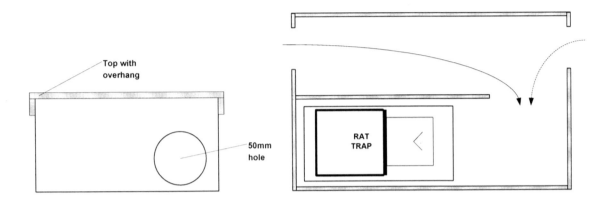

Alternative 'Double' box

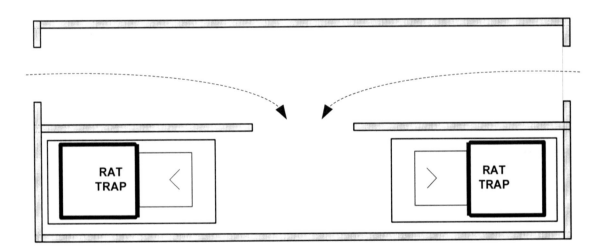

Further Resources

www.fourteenacre.co.uk
The companion website to this book contains a range of photographs and information. Any updates will be published here along with feedback, suggestions and experience from other people who have bought and used the book.
Accessories and trap components are also available from this site.

Camp Life in the Woods and the Tricks of Trapping and Trap Making
by William Hamilton Gibson.
An incredibly detailed and varied catalogue of designs and descriptions of 19th Century traps, many of which are no longer legal to use.
Available as a free eBook from Project Gutenberg.
http://www.gutenberg.org/files/17093/17093-h/17093-h.htm
Also available as a print to order book from multiple suppliers on Amazon but ensure you order the illustrated version.

Trap Making Primitive & Modern
Burt, Monro, Massey (& Stromberg)
A collection of schematic line drawings of many trap types.
Available in the UK on ebay or from www.fourteenacre.co.uk

Rabbit Control
By Jackie Drakeford
Published by Swan Hill Press
An all round guide to rabbit control including a very good chapter on 'field to table'.

Trapping, A Practical Guide
By James A. Bateman
Part history, part practical, a guide to many types of trap and their use.
Published by David and Charles

The Smallholders DIY
By Michael Roberts, Golden Cockerel Series
Only one item in this book to do with trapping; a box for Fenn traps. However it's full of other simple but effective woodwork projects for the small holder.

Notes

Notes

Notes

Lightning Source UK Ltd.
Milton Keynes UK
01 January 2009
148079UK00001B/3/P

9 780955 853500